THE DOMINO EFFECT

FALLING FORWARD INTO THE STORY OF GOOD AND EVIL

THE DOMINO EFFECT

FALLING FORWARD INTO THE STORY OF GOOD AND EVIL

WAYFARER

CHRIS BROOKS

CHAD NORRIS

DAVE RHODES

THOMAS NELSON

Since 1798

NASHVILLE   DALLAS   MEXICO CITY   RIO DE JANEIRO   BEIJING

Published in Nashville, Tennessee, by Thomas Nelson. Thomas Nelson is a trademark of Thomas Nelson, Inc.

Thomas Nelson, Inc. titles may be purchased in bulk for educational, business, fund-raising, or sales promotional use. For information, please e-mail SpecialMarkets@thomasnelson.com.

Special thanks to Tony Campolo for the use of his statement, "It's Friday, but Sunday's comin'."

Scripture quotations are taken from The Voice™ translation. Copyright © 2006, 2007, 2008 by Ecclesia Bible Society. Used by permission. All rights reserved.

ISBN 978-1-4185-3341-0

Printed in the United States of America

08 09 10 11 12 RRD 9 8 7 6 5 4 3 2 1

To those who know there **must** be more . . .
but have not found it **yet** . . .

CONTENTS

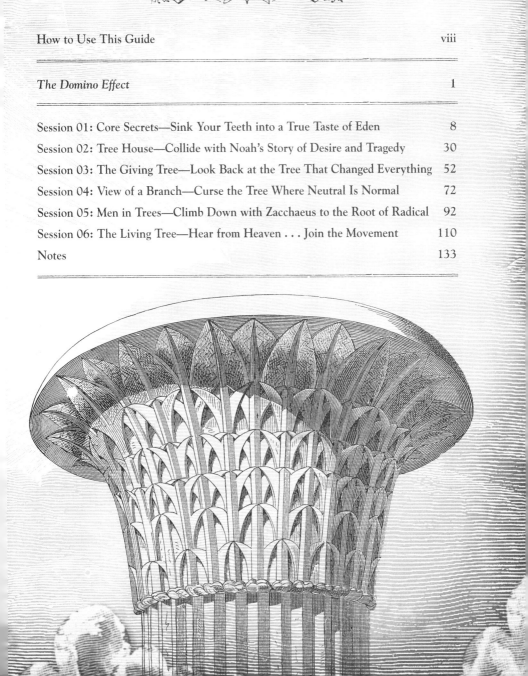

HOW TO USE THIS GUIDE

The Participant's Guide is an integral part of the *Domino Effect* experience designed to facilitate your small group gatherings with directed questions and content drivers, while also providing a steady influx of devotional and missional supplements throughout the week. The Participant's Guide is broken into six chapters that correspond to each DVD session. Each chapter has two parts: the video discussion and the daily readings.

The Video Discussion

We understand that the quality of questions is just as important as the content that preceded them. A strong desire to create dynamic small group discussion times and foster an authentic community experience led us to create a video discussion piece that strategically summarizes key points, scripture verses, and illustrations from each session, and then crafts pertinent, open-ended questions designed to invite you to engage your story with God's story.

The Daily Readings

Even if you have the most incredible small group times watching the session and processing the questions, inevitably you have to wait about seven days before you meet again, thus losing key momentum and valuable traction. In the past, small group curriculum has offered you two options to help bridge the weeklong gap: a workbook or nothing. Nothing didn't work, and the workbook was great for the people who had the time and endurance for that kind of study. But for those of us who find time a precious commodity, we wound up doing a week's worth of workbook work twenty minutes before

the next small group session so we wouldn't feel too guilty. We decided to take a different approach with this study.

The daily readings are written as a compact devotional guide customized to flow right out of your small group time and into the next session. Written by the same speakers from the DVD sessions, with the scripture printed right there and an easy reference back to key points and questions from the video session, the daily readings allow you to marinate your heart and mind at strategic touch points throughout the week. And just in case you can't find the time to read or if you actually prefer listening, each Participant's Guide features an audio companion with MP3 versions of each daily devotional. Professionally scored, read by the featured speakers from the DVD sessions, and narrated with the listener-friendly Voice translation of the Bible, you can listen by uploading the audio files into iTunes or a similar MP3 player. (Other format players can be used by transferring the files to a new CD.)

By 12:28

A distinct feature found in the daily readings and audio companion is a segment entitled *By 12:28*. Taken as a play on words from our product line, Room 1228, *By 12:28* refers to awareness of one's limited amount of time to act and make a difference in the domino effect. At the end of each daily segment, there is an innovative challenge for you to complete before the clock strikes 12:28 the next day. Some days these challenges are internal and reflective, like plotting key moments in your own story that have shaped who you are today. At other times they are intentionally missional but tactfully simple, like buying a friend lunch. This shared sense of mission and activity provides you a connection to the group and the *Domino Effect* experience throughout the week without bogging you down or overwhelming you with an impossible workload. *By 12:28* provides each person with a sense of ownership and individuality while serving as a great conversation starter to your next session.

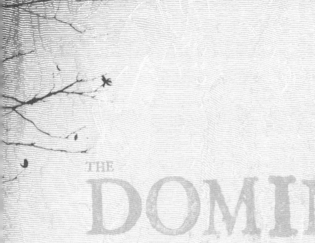

THE DOMINO EFFECT

FALLING FORWARD INTO THE STORY OF GOOD AND EVIL

The Domino Effect

The Domino Effect
It's a tale of trees rooted in history
His story, that is, of good and evil
    God and man
        Planned parenthood
           No yin and no yang

But a tale told true:
We weren't set up to be messed up
    But we messed up what God set up

The vile of evil cracks open
It floods like a cancer through creation's blood cells
So with tears in His eyes and dirt underneath His fingernails
God floods back
    He floods back
        To stack
           His creation against the evil that attacks
             But the seismic impact
               Has already cracked
                 The foundation of the human
                   heart

And even though Noah's tree house lands safely

The dominos continue to **fall**

The dominos continue to drop

Evil did its worst

All the dominos crushed the cartilage of a dead rabbi

Hanging from a dead tree

It was finished

It was paid for

It was Friday

It was Friday

It was Friday

It was Friday, but Sunday was a-comin'

And the insurrection of the resurrection had begun

Tick tock, tick tock

Death had begun to die

Tick tock, tick tock

Redemption is rolling up its sleeves and taking off its tie

Tick tock, tick tock

Spring has sprung

And from out of Eden's twilight

Here comes our cry:

"EVIL, let us LIVE!"

Because all in all
You're just another brick in the wall
      That is cracked
           And crumbling
               And decaying
Every time the church is saying,
"Christ is crucified"
"Christ is risen"
And "Christ is coming"
Again and again and again and again
We sing it
      We preach it
           We dance it
              We whisper it to ourselves
                 . . . Twice daily

But we still, still have a fig tree with no figs
A temple with no tact
A religion with no regard
And a bunch of services, but no servants
      Willing to take care of the widow, the orphan, and the
          foreigner

So Jesus said in the King James Version,
"Bump dat and flip dat house
Upside down and inside out"
Forcing us to see
That sometimes
The way up is to go down
And sometimes
The way to grasp your life
Is to **Let go of it**

Let Go of your adult sensibilities and see a piece of God
In a child's sense of wonder and willingness to dream
Then a piece of God might be seen
In a grown, short man
Climbing a poor tree
Dumbstruck, Zacchaeus had to be asking,
>"How can it be
>That Thou, my God, would dine with me?"

So the dominos continue to fall
The dominos continue to drop
>Forward into the story of good and evil
Two stories clickety-clacketing forward
In a furious race for your time
Begging you not to pantomime
>Religious rules and regulations
>Or mirrored regurgitations
But giving everything you've got
It may not be much
It may not be mulch
But a decision must be made today and every day

Because no good—
>That's not good
And not good is evil
That is to say, neutrality
That's no longer an option
And much to our dismay
Jesus—He's still on His way

***

HEAVEN IS COMING TO EARTH

Jesus is coming again
And the insurrection of the resurrection will be ushered in
The dissection of the body and soul
Finally will be made whole
And reunite at the intersection
Of the tree of life and the throne of the living God

Oh, no longer will we settle for just a piece of God
We will live, breathe, thrive, dance, serve, eat, drink—deeply
Of the 100 proof
        Undistilled peace of God that passes all understanding
That is now demanding

That I stand to my feet on resurrected **earth**
For a tectonic shift has occurred
The continental drift is deterred
And a supersonic shout can be heard:
        "Now the dwelling of God is with man"

Therefore let us pass the **peace**

The eschatological center of gravity is here
The polarity of my magnetized longings I will no longer fear
For they are now connected in God's new clear

Family

But for a moment in time I imagine that I am given this revelation
    divine
And when I see that He's gonna wipe every tear from their

eye

I feel compelled and propelled to call a time out and wonder
Why would anyone on resurrected earth have reason to shed tears?

Perhaps then a rumbling whisper would say,
"They weep for the lost seconds, minutes, and days
That were spent during their first life
Blinded by a temporary glare
Obscuring the reality that

    My **power**
      My presence
      My peace
Had always been available to them
Right then and right there"

So I drop to my knees
And I begin to plead
With the words of an old hymn

And heaven's decree:

"This is my Father's world
O let me ne'er forget
That though the wrong
Seems oft so strong
God is the Ruler yet

I say this is my Father's world
The battle is not done
Jesus who died will be satisfied

WHEN
EARTH
AND
HEAVEN
BECOME
ONE."

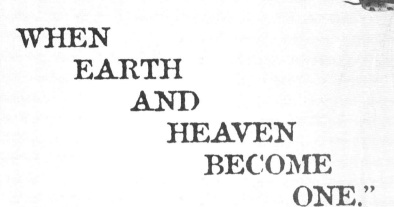

THE
DOMINO
EFFECT

FALLING FORWARD INTO THE STORY OF GOOD AND EVIL

7

SESSION

01

Core Secrets

Video Discussion

**We weren't set up to be messed up, but we messed up
what God set up.**

It's an awareness we come to gradually—the knowledge of evil in the world. It's a moment that, once you see it, colors the way you see everything else after it. It can be planes flying into buildings on 9/11, or someone with the full use of his legs blatantly parking in a handicapped parking spot during the crowded holiday season. It could be parents getting a divorce, or someone stealing something precious to you.

> **"The Domino Effect**
>
> **It's a tale of trees rooted in
> history
> His story, that is, of good and
> evil
> God and man
> Planned parenthood
> No yin and no yang**
>
> **But a tale told true:
> We weren't set up to be
> messed up
> But we messed up what
> God set up."**

When were your eyes first opened to the struggle of good versus evil in the world?

God isn't setting us up to fail—like an existential game of Kerplunk or a spiritual game of Jenga. God is not just waiting for us to pull the wrong straw and have our lives come crashing down around us. But this is how many of us see Him. We feel we need to walk on eggshells, fearing that He is hovering over us, waiting for us to ruin our lives.

 How have you struggled with distorted pictures of God?

God gave Adam both freedom and authority in the garden of Eden. The Garden was good but not perfect. Adam and Eve were expected to contribute; they were told to work the Garden. God has given you great freedom and great responsibility and authority as well. He's not hovering over us, looking for us to do right and wrong. He gives us freedom in our relationship with Him.

 How did you feel hearing Dave repeat, "You are free" over and over? Did you think of any particular event or circumstance in your history as he emphasized this?

Genesis 2:8–9, 15–17 (The Voice)

The Eternal God planted a garden in the east and called it Eden—for it was a place of utter delight—and placed the man there. In this garden He made the ground pregnant with life—bursting forth with nourishing food and luxuriant beauty. He created trees that ravished the eyes and yielded unimaginable delicacies.

Among them stood the tree of life. And in the center of this garden of delights stood the tree of the knowledge of good and evil. . . . The Eternal God placed the man in the garden of Eden with a prime directive: conserve and conceive. Work the ground for your sustenance and conserve, care for, and carry on that which you have been given. Eat freely from any and all trees in the garden. I only require that you abstain from eating the fruit of one tree—the tree of knowledge of good and evil. Beware: the day you eat the fruit of this tree, you will die.

11

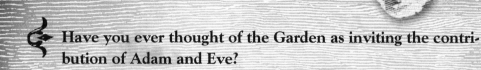

 Have you ever thought of the Garden as inviting the contribution of Adam and Eve?

God's job is to make value judgments about what is good and true—and what is not. Our job is to trust Him to have our best interests at heart. But Adam and Eve made a fatal decision: to rely on their own value judgment, not God's. They messed up what God set up. Adam and Eve were just trying to LIVE, but what they did turned out to be EVIL.

 When were you just trying to live only to "get to the other side of the glass" and then realized that it was evil?

God gave Adam and Eve the tree of life and the Tree of Knowledge of Good and Evil to give them, and us, an opportunity to join in His goodness. In fact, it's not about the trees at all—it's about the heartbeat of God. Instead of viewing God as someone who is just setting us up for failure, we need to recognize that He is setting us up for freedom and delight. But the journey still continues today—it didn't end with Adam and Eve.

 How is Adam's and Eve's story your story?

 Right now, is your life or circumstance more caught up in the domino effect of evil or good?

DAY 1: Created for Blessing

by Dave Rhodes

When was the last time you were with someone who just didn't get it? You know the person we're talking about—someone who is oblivious to something that seems obvious to you, someone who is confused by what is clear to everyone else, someone who just can't see the eight-hundred-pound gorilla standing in the room.

Or maybe there's a better question: When was the last time that person was *you*?

In 2007 the *Washington Post* conducted a social experiment. A reporter got the world-class violinist, Joshua Bell, to spend a morning during rush hour playing at a Washington, D.C., metro station. The reporter had two questions as he watched to see if anyone noticed this beautiful art on display: (1) Would the beauty of Bell's music transcend a mundane setting and an inconvenient time?, and (2) How would people react to beautiful art when that art is found in a not-so-beautiful environment?

Bell, who was dressed in street clothes and had an open violin case beside him, played six classical pieces over forty-three minutes. The reporter counted 1,097 people who walked by. Twenty-seven gave Bell money, totaling thirty-two dollars and some change. Only seven stopped what they were doing to hang around and listen to part of the performance. The vast majority of people were so wrapped up in their own cares, worries, and business that they missed what was right in front of them. Others were listening to music on their iPods and never even heard Bell's beautiful music. Still others heard, but were ignorant of the quality of what they were hearing.

Whatever their reasons, it's amazing to think about just how many people missed the beauty that was in their presence that day. Joshua Bell plays at night to sold-out concert halls filled with people who pay hundreds of dollars to hear him and stand to applaud when he is done. But that morning in the D.C. metro station, this same man, performing the same songs he performs each night, managed to have only seven people pause even for a minute. He received not a single hand clap and just thirty-two bucks as he stood and played his violin for anyone who would listen.

The reporter writing the article came to a fascinating conclusion. Based on this experiment, he determined that people fail to recognize beauty. In other words, most people have to be told that something is beautiful before they see it. We have a hard time recognizing beauty on our own. To put it another way, we are all oblivious to what should be obvious to us.[1]

Genesis 1:31–2:3 (The Voice):

Narrator: Then God surveyed everything He had created thus far, *savoring its beauty and* appreciating its goodness.

Evening gave way to morning on day six.

So now you see how the Creator swept into being the spangled heavens and earth *in six days.* The canvas of the cosmos was completed by day seven, when the True God paused the labor of creating and rested. Thus the Creator blessed day seven *as an open space* designed for rest and relaxation, *a sacred zone of Sabbath-keeping, because God rested from His work that day.*

In these verses, we catch God just after He completed His creative work. The words we read here come following the sixth day of creation, as God forms man and woman from the dust of the ground with His own hands and His own breath. Here, God stands and blesses His creation, breaking from His creative rhythm just long enough to declare His handiwork not just good, but *very* good. He asks man and woman to share in this goodness. But to do so, they will have to continually recognize the beauty of God's created order.

God did not set us up to be messed up.

He set us up for blessing.

He set us up to share in His goodness.

He set us up to live in His favor.

He set us up to be His partners in His beautiful world.

Sadly, however, the beauty of the picture we find in Genesis 1 is soon traded in Genesis 3 for a disturbing picture of brokenness. By following their own way, Adam and Eve messed up what God set up, missing the beauty in their midst and therefore trading that beauty for the beast we now know as brokenness and evil. In their story, we find our own story as well.

What beauty did you see or discover this week?

Here's Your Challenge— Now You're on the Clock

By 12:28 tomorrow, honor something beautiful. Be on the lookout for beauty in your midst. Whether it's a sunset, a work of art, the talent of another human being, or the manifested presence of God that comes to us in hundreds of ways each day, honor this beauty by taking time to pause and stand in amazement. Clap if the moment seems right. Gasp if that seems better. Then let someone else know about the beauty you see.

DAY 2: Created for Intimacy

by Chris Brooks

Shhhh . . .

Don't move a muscle.
Don't make a sound.
Don't even breathe.
Stay hidden at all costs.

Do you remember the electricity you felt when you played hide-and-seek? Do you remember the thrill of seeing someone's feet slowly pass by you, the agony of trying to stay motionless and silent, and the euphoric fright and subsequent utter delight you felt when you were called out of your dark hiding place by the seeker?

One thing you soon realize when you play this game is that hide-and-seek only works if the seeker is actually seeking you. Yesterday we saw the core secret that God didn't set us up to be messed up—He created Adam and Eve for blessing. Today we will see that God also created *us* for intimacy and that He is constantly seeking us so that we can live in this intimacy with Him.

Genesis 1:27–28 (The Voice):

Narrator: So God created humans in His own image. He created them male and female in His own image, *reflecting God's own relational richness.* Then God blessed humans.

God: *Continue My creativity! The world needs your tender care and cultivation.* Be productive. Have children so you can stretch out across this world. Rule the fish of the sea, the birds of the air, and every specimen of creation, *even the earth itself.*

Genesis 3:8 (The Voice):

Just then, they heard the Eternal God walking in the cool shadows of the garden. They took cover among the trees.

We weren't set up to be messed up. Instead, God set us up for blessing and intimacy. He created a place where man and woman could know Him freely, walk with Him in the cool of the day, and experience the utter delight of getting to learn and live and love in this relationship and environment. We were set up for intimacy with God and with each other.

So why is God so often portrayed as a prudish, old fuddy-duddy who is almost embarrassed about human intimacy and sexuality? After all, the story of Eden says that the first thing God tells Adam and Eve to do is to do *it*—to conceive. This creative collision of divine intimacy, human sexuality, and loyal commitment shows us that God didn't set us up to be messed up, but somehow we messed up what God set up. Adam and Eve short-circuited God's ecology of trust and obedience—the place where real intimacy and delight occurs—by breaking through the only boundary line that their Creator had given them.

Yet even after this betrayal cracked the created order, we see God still actively seeking intimacy with His children. While Adam and Eve took cover and hid in the trees as they became encased in their fear and shame, God still sought them. He called out to ask, "Where are you?" And even though we, too, mess up what God set up, and there will be grave consequences for both God and man because of how we let evil break into our stories, God still seeks after us with an unflinching, unwavering desire for intimacy. He wants us to stop hiding *from* Him and start hiding *in* Him.

12:28 by
Here's Your Challenge—
Now You're on the Clock

By 12:28 tomorrow, hide in God. Find a place to take cover in Him. Go under a blanket, in a closet, or even under a bed—just get in a place where the physical space reminds you of the truth that God created you for intimacy and that, through Jesus Christ, you are now hidden in God. Spend five minutes or fifteen minutes or however long it takes to come before God like a child who withholds nothing, confesses everything, and trusts with reckless abandon that you are surrounded and enveloped by a love beyond description.

DAY 3: Created for Purpose

by Chris Brooks

What are three things you would do with a million dollars?

1. _____
2. _____
3. _____

If you are like me, you have a couple of prepackaged, stock answers for this question, because you have secretly planned for (and maybe even prayed for) such a day of unexpected financial bliss and blessing. My first three answers to this question are automatic at this point:

1. Pay off student loans.
2. Pay off the house.
3. Get a family car that doesn't leak oil like the Exxon *Valdez*.

It's fun to daydream about what we would do with a million dollars, because this scenario seems to have the promise of solving all of our problems. But many lottery winners find out that this isn't the case at all. For example, Bud Post won $16.2 million in the Pennsylvania lottery in 1988. Fewer than twenty years later, he had been through several lawsuits, had declared bankruptcy, and lived off his $450 monthly Social Security check and food stamps. Suzanne Mullins won $4.2 million in the Virginia lottery in 1993, but by 2006 owed more than $1 million to a company that had advanced her a loan against her yearly payments. Worst of all, Evelyn Adams, who won the New Jersey lottery not once, but twice, amassing a total of $5.4 million in winnings in the mid-1980s, lost much of her money playing slot machines in Atlantic City. She is now broke and living in a trailer.[2]

I reference these million-dollar tragedies to show that without a purpose or plan, all of us run the risk of bankrupting what we have been given. That's what happened to Adam and Eve. God had given them great power, blessing, intimacy, and authority. He also gave them a great purpose on which to focus their resources. That purpose? Caring for and continuing God's creation. In short, their job was to conserve and conceive. God created Adam and Eve (and us) to have work, to have a purpose, to matter, and to function within His created order.

Without this great sense of purpose or an identity as co-workers with God, we will inevitably bankrupt His blessing by spending it in foolish and careless ways. This is one of the core secrets the early church tapped into. Let's see how Luke described this community's shared sense of purpose and their passion for that purpose.

Acts 2:42–47 (The Voice):

The community continually committed themselves to learning what the apostles taught them, gathering for fellowship, breaking the bread, and praying. Everyone felt a sense of awe because the Lord's emissaries were doing many signs and wonders among them. There was an intense sense of togetherness among all who believed; they shared all their material possessions in trust. They sold any possessions and goods *that did not benefit the community* and used the money to help everyone in need. They were unified as they worshiped at the temple day after day. In homes, they broke bread and shared meals with glad and generous hearts. The new disciples praised God, and they enjoyed the goodwill of all the people *of the city*. Day after day the Lord added to their number everyone who was experiencing liberation.

Great purpose must accompany great power and great blessing, or else these gifts will become self-destructive. God created us to create. He created Adam and Eve with the purpose of caring for the Garden and for each other. Likewise, in Acts we see the church caring for each other and cultivating an environment in which people could once again delight in God and share in His goodness through Jesus, the Liberating King. We see here how God created a nation of priests, through the unifying power of the Holy Spirit, in order to conserve, care for, and carry on the gospel message.

12:28 by Here's Your Challenge— Now You're on the Clock

By 12:28 tomorrow, spend it like you've got it. Spend some of your time, money, or talents to bless someone in your small group or circle of friends. Take what God has blessed you with to conserve, care for, and cultivate an intense sense of togetherness by sharing a meal, an act of service, or any other creative act. As you do this, remember that you are liberating yourself and someone else with this powerful sense of purpose and passion.

DAY 4: Created for Authority

by Chad Norris

"Sam? Sam! It's time to eat. Sit down at the table, son."

"Sam? Sam! It's time to take a bath. Let's go!"

"Load up in the car, Sam. It's time to go to school."

Whenever I say something like this, I realize that I am a parent and that I have authority over my son. Man, it feels good. Now that I have two kids, the idea of authority has become a reality in my life. I now have authority over four-year-old Sam and his sister, Ruthie. It's a strange thought, to be honest with you. But it's extremely natural.

I tell Sam and Ruthie when to go to bed, when to eat, and when to play. Pretty much everything in their lives revolves around what my wife and I tell them to do. I have authority over my children, and my wife has authority over me. (Guys, you understand what I'm talking about.)

Genesis 2:19 (The Voice):

Out of the *same* ground that the man came from, the Eternal God sculpted animals and birds of every kind. Then He brought them to the man and gave him the authority to name each creature as he saw fit, *thereby making room for humans to participate in God's creative act.*

It's funny how some truths in the Word of God just slide by us. If I were to ask you who named all the animals, you would probably say that God did it. But that's not what happened. God put Adam in the Garden and gave him the job of naming the animals.

You might wonder why it even matters that Adam named the animals. It's because this shows us just how much authority God gave this man. The whole earth was and is God's, and that means everything in the Garden was God's. But God chose to give Adam authority to rule over the Garden and tend it. He gave Adam the authority to name the animals. God created Adam for authority, and He set us up for authority as well. But too often, we miss the truth that God set us up for astounding authority, and we mess up what God set up.

So what does this mean in our lives? For my wife and me as we raise our kids, our goal is not to abuse authority, but to instead use our authority to bless our children's lives. Likewise, we can abuse power, but we can also use it for tremendous good. And that's what God is after. He wants His people to have the authority to dream, imagine, explore, and create. Even Jesus reminds us that He has all authority and gives us that authority to share the good news of the gospel (Matthew 28:18–20).

by 12:2₈ Here's Your Challenge— Now You're on the Clock

By 12:28 tomorrow, name an animal—whatever that means in your life. Are you daring to dream about how you can use the authority God has given you? Are you using that authority to unleash good in the world? Or have you allowed the evil around you to keep you from experiencing the authority for which God has created you? Wrestle with these questions, and then find one way to exercise the authority God has given you—just like Adam did when he named the animals.

DAY 5: We Messed Up

by Dave Rhodes

Naked is awkward. In fact, I bet you're having an awkward moment right now just reading the word naked during your devotion time. Whether it is physical, emotional, or social, most of us are uncomfortable being naked and exposed for the world to see.

The whole naked thing happened to me on vacation last summer. Allow me to explain: I was in Myrtle Beach, South Carolina. Some people call Myrtle Beach the Redneck Riviera, so a naked moment probably shouldn't have surprised me, but it did. By Thursday of my weeklong vacation, I was in my morning routine of waking up late, going for a jog, grabbing a late-morning snack, and meeting my family at the pool. When I got to the pool, my wife asked me to take our daughter, Emma, back up to our room on the tenth floor to get something that she forgot. Being the incredibly gracious husband that I am, I quickly agreed to do my fatherly duty.

Knowing that I had some time to kill in transit, I called Chad Norris to catch up. I was on my cell phone, and Emma was right beside me. When we got to the elevator, I let Emma press the button, since she loves to push buttons so much. The elevator door opened, and Emma and I got on. Then Emma pressed the button for our floor. I was still talking to Norris when the elevator doors opened and Emma and I got off. We walked down the hall to our room like we always did and opened the unlocked door. But once we got into the room, I noticed something wasn't right. The room was laid out the same, but the furniture looked different. I couldn't figure out what was going on—until I saw some guy I didn't know lying on the couch. He was wearing boxer shorts and nothing else.

Picture the scene: I was on the phone, and my four-year-old daughter and I were staring at a half-naked man in front of us. My mind couldn't wrap itself around what was happening, and so we all stared at each other for thirty seconds. (In case you don't know, thirty seconds is a really long time to stare at a half-naked man.) Then it hit me: I was in the wrong condo. Somehow, Emma and I had gotten off the elevator three floors too early. We had walked into someone else's room, and now we were staring at someone else's nakedness. To be honest, I was feeling pretty naked myself. I quickly said hello, explained the situation, and walked out of the room, feeling more than a little embarrassed, hoping that I never bumped into this half-naked man again.

 Have you ever had a time when you felt naked like this? What happened?

Think back today to that moment of nakedness as you read the story of how God found Adam and Eve in *their* naked moment.

Genesis 3:7–13 (The Voice):

Narrator: Suddenly their eyes were opened *to a reality previously unknown.* For the first time, they *sensed their vulnerability and rushed* to hide their naked bodies, stitching fig leaves into a crude loincloth. Just then, they heard the Eternal God walking in the cool shadows of the garden. They took cover among the trees.

Eternal God *(calling to the man)*: Where are you?

Man: I was hiding from You. I was afraid when I heard You coming.

Eternal God: *Why are you afraid?*

Man: Because I am naked.

Eternal God: Who told you that you are naked? Have you eaten from the tree *in the center of the garden,* the one I commanded you not to eat from?

Man *(pointing at the woman)*: *It was she!* The woman You gave to me put the fruit in my hands, and I ate it.

Eternal God *(to the woman)*: What have you done?

Woman: It was the serpent! He tricked me, and I ate.

You've read all week about how we weren't set up to be messed up, but we messed up what God set up. Unfortunately, mess comes with consequences. In this passage, the nakedness that had once been normal now became awkward, and Adam's and Eve's eyes were opened. Because of their sin, they now needed clothes that would both cover them and also restrain them.

But fig-leaf garments weren't the only things that cloaked their bodies. All that Adam and Eve were created for was now covered as well. Their authority was now shrouded, because they challenged God's authority. Their intimacy was now veiled by shame. Their purpose was now masked by insecurity, and their blessing was hidden by a curse.

The fallout of them messing up was not simply that the world was broken; it was that the man and woman were broken and, even more, that *we* are now broken. We find ourselves hardwired for more than we experience. Now, things like authority and intimacy and purpose seem awkward at best to us. And when we stare at God, we feel . . . *well, naked.* It wasn't supposed to be this way.

12:28 Here's Your Challenge— Now You're on the Clock

By 12:28 tomorrow, get naked. Not physically, but spiritually. Make a list below of things that are covering authority, intimacy, and purpose in your life. Think about the things that cause you shame and insecurity. Spend a moment of awkwardness undressing these things in your life while you stare at God. Then take one of these places of shame or insecurity and uncover it to a trusted friend who can help you once again hear the rhythm of grace in your life.

SESSION

Tree House

Collide with Noah's Story of Desire and Tragedy

Video Discussion

Good stories tell of the collision between what you want and what you got.

The tree house: it's symbolic of the moment that forever changed you. It was freedom and adventure. It was where you went to let your imagination run wild. You could get out of your family tree and into a new place where you were the king or queen of the castle, and you had a cast of characters who did exactly what you wanted them to do. Your every desire came true!

 Where did you go as a kid to escape from reality—to daydream, to plan, to imagine the world as you wanted it to be?

"The vile of evil cracks open
It floods like a cancer through
    creation's blood cells
So with tears in His eyes and dirt
    underneath His fingernails
God floods back
  He floods back
    To stack
        His creation against the
            evil that attacks
        But the seismic impact
        Has already cracked
            The foundation of
                the human
                heart
And even though Noah's tree
    house lands safely
The dominos continue to fall
The dominos continue to drop."

This week, you will look back at the key events in your life. Moments of good and evil advanced your story. This complex mixture has charted your course; it has written the themes of your life. Your faith is grown out of this story, a response to God's hand moving among the desires and tragedies of your journey.

 Can you imagine that great passion can come from great pain? In what places have you seen this to be true in your story?

Your faith is shaped by the environment in which you grew up. Your family and those close to you spoke into your life from the day you were born, and some of the baggage and beauty they owned seeped down into your psyche. As a child, you were defenseless against its influence. Thankfully, some of us came from good homes and good lives. Our faiths were crafted in climate-controlled environments. Mostly good things happened to us. Others of us were not so lucky.

 Talk about the environment you grew up in.

Eventually, evil comes crashing in and chaos rains down on all of us. God does not protect us from the story of evil: divorce, death, injury, betrayal, illness, abandonment. At some point, something happened that changed *your* story. A plot twist occurred that you never expected, and you would never be the same again. This series is about courageously revisiting those moments.

What was the moment that forever changed you? When did tragedy (evil) intersect with your desires?

Genesis 6:5–13 (The Voice)

Narrator: The Eternal God saw evil rampaging throughout the earth. When He decided that wickedness had become the all-consuming human addiction, His heart broke. The Eternal was sorry He had ever created humanity to live on His perfect earth.

Eternal God: *What have I done in creating and loving this human?*

Narrator: *The more God pondered how to minimize the damage, the more He determined to unmake what He had made.*

Eternal God: I'll erase the humans I've created and all the companions I made for them—animals, insects, and birds—from the land because I am sorry that I ever made them.

Narrator: But there was one human whom the Eternal God could not let go of—Noah—because this man pleased Him. This is the story of Noah and his descendants: Noah was a good man, blameless among the people of his time, and Noah walked with God. Noah had three sons: Shem, Ham, and Japheth.

God saw that the earth was vile and violent. God recognized that His perfect earth was rotting because of humanity's putrid actions.

Eternal God *(to Noah)*: I am ready to erase all flesh. *They have turned the planet's ecosystem into an egosystem;* humans cannot stop defiling each other and the home I made for them. *I'm done.* I will use the earth to ruin them *as they have rotted the earth.*

If you could, would you take some of the painful and tragic chapters out of your life? How would you be different if you did?

Despite the mess mankind made of God's plan to love and bless humanity, God was not sorry He made man—He was sorry for what man made of himself. God knew He had to follow the path of justice with a world gone mad, but it broke His heart to do so.

Chris related the story of Noah's tragedy to that of having to put down his beloved dog, Albus. His grief is genuine even now, years later, as he remembers leaving his dog at the humane shelter that day with the words "Daddy loves you." He said that this experience gave him insight into the breaking heart of God during the time of Noah.

 In what ways do you think God's discipline in your life hurts Him more than it hurts you?

Evil has touched all of us in some way, but before we can dress our wounds, we have to stop the bleeding. And the only way to deal with our grief is to grieve. We must permit and promote a faith structure that allows us to experience grief and anger, rather than skipping ahead to redemption. Warm and fuzzy verses taken out of context are not only empty platitudes; they're dangerous and potentially catastrophic theological statements that short-circuit the grieving process and encourage repression and outright rebellion.

 When has the power of presence—of someone simply sitting and sharing your pain—transformed your life?

 How is it "potentially catastrophic" to take verses out of context and skip ahead to redemption when someone you know is grieving the effects of evil in his or her life?

Sometimes evil chooses us—such as the death of a loved one or the divorce of parents. Other times we choose our own evil. But it's critical that we have the courage to name the evil in our journey—that's what makes it real and allows us to deal with it. It's profoundly difficult, but it's profoundly necessary.

 What issues exist in your family tree?

 How can you avoid passing on the evil that has been passed down to you?

We deal with evil in our lives by either making excuses for it or by really dealing with it. There may be plenty of legitimate reasons for the evil in our lives, but making excuses will never help us. When you name your evil and wipe it clean, you eliminate the shame that seeks control of your heart. True freedom comes with confession—handing your tragedies over to God.

 How can you hand your tragedies to God right now?

 What can you do at a practical level to deny evil power in your life and wipe it clean?

Daily Readings

DAY 1: Naming Evil

by Chris Brooks

What one poor farm boy wanted was to be a lawyer. What he got was an unjust prison sentence of twenty-seven years. From this collision unfolds the good story of civil rights hero Nelson Mandela.

What one wealthy Southern girl wanted was a perfect childhood. What she got was scarlet fever, which left her deaf and blind. From this collision unfolds the good story of Helen Keller, the first deaf and blind person to graduate from college.

What one man wanted was to preach to troops in the Korean army. What he got was a check for fifty dollars and an overwhelming burden for children orphaned by war. From this collision unfolds the good story of international poverty abolitionist Everett Swanson and his organization, Compassion International.

Good stories tell of the intersection between what you want and what you got. This is true of our story and of our Creator's story as well. What God wanted was to bless humanity and share His divine intimacy, purpose, and authority with His people. But what God got from mankind was tragically different. You and I were born into this intersection, this tension between God's desire to know and love and redeem His creation, and the tragedy of our stubborn refusal to be part of His story. We can see the plot unfold as desire and tragedy collide in Noah's story as well.

Noah was a good man, blameless among the people of his time, and he became a key player in the story of good and evil. But even after saving the future of humanity and the entire animal kingdom, narrowly escaping cataclysmic destruction by the grace of God, and surviving the worst family cruise ever taken, Noah walked out of his floating tree house only to be hit upside the head by his own family tree. Noah got hammered by a two-by-four of evil as something really strange and especially shameful happened.

Genesis 9:20–23 (The Voice):

Noah, *a gardener at heart, conceived a vinery.* He planted and harvested the vineyard, *allowed the grapes to ferment into wine, and* then enjoyed an exuberant amount of his first vintage. After Noah collapsed in a drunken heap inside his tent, his son Ham, the father of Canaan, snuck a peek at his exposed father and summoned his two brothers *to laugh with him at their father's nakedness. Instead of looking and laughing,* Shem and Japheth took a cloak, laid it across their shoulders, walked backward *into the tent* never looking behind, and covered their father's nakedness. They closed their eyes to their father's embarrassment.

I have to say that I'm glad Noah's drunkenness never got rebuked, because if anyone on the face of the earth—which at that point was just he and seven family members—deserved a drink, it was this guy. This claustrophobic zookeeper managed to save his family from an evil population only to discover that his son snuck some of that evil aboard the ark because it was stowed away in his heart.

This passage is cryptic about the nature of Ham's transgression. Opinions of modern scholars all the way back to Jewish sages abound, from something as simple as childish mockery to much darker speculations. But regardless of the transgression or Noah's condition, the emphasis is on Ham's reaction to his father's nakedness. This son took an outspoken delight in his father's shame and made no effort to alleviate it or cover it up.

All of us have cryptic and shameful chapters in our lives, and we must practice calculated vulnerability and steer clear of those who would delight in or diminish the pain and hurt with which our experiences have marked us. If we are to follow the bold example of this passage, we need to name these moments of evil in our stories.

God can take what was meant for evil and turn it into good—but not until it has been named, confronted, confessed, and exposed to His healing, redemptive hand. Some moments are horrible and obvious, such as death or incidents of sexual abuse. Some moments are as subtle and common as being bullied or falsely accused. Offhanded comments can be seared into our psyches so that they fester for years. And neglect can be the most subtle and devastating form of abuse, because it leads you to believe the lie that no one cares.

No matter the situation, decay violently cracks through our families and communities in tragic ways. But today is a pivotal point in our stories. We all need to name these moments and identify their settings, characters, dialogue, and impact. Doing this exercise requires enormous honesty and courage, yet it is the only way we can move deeper into the plot of the story of good in our lives.

12:28 Here's Your Challenge— Now You're on the Clock

By 12:28 tomorrow, plot your own story. Draw a line or the arc (no pun intended) of your life story below. Include key moments of good and evil that advanced the story and created the themes of your life. Most of us will discover that our passion and purpose in life come from a complex mixture of good and evil. As you plot your story, ask God to reveal the dominant themes and hidden plot twists that might have eluded you.

DAY 2: Evil Inherited

by Dave Rhodes

A few months ago, my dad got a new TV. In most families, this purchase wouldn't be that big of a deal. But in my family, this is almost on the same level as Moses parting the Red Sea. Growing up, we had the same TV for as long as I can remember, and it wasn't a good one. You could describe the television experience at my house as "thirteen inches of haze."

As if that wasn't bad enough, my dad insisted on inviting people over to the house to watch sports or movies with him. We hosted I-don't-know-how-many parties where groups of people huddled around this miniature TV to see if the wide receiver caught the pass or the last-second shot actually went in.

So when my dad called to tell me about his new TV, you can imagine the pride in his voice. He used words like "big screen," "flat screen," and "high-definition," which filled me with confidence that this new advancement in technology would change his life. (I didn't have the heart to tell him that thirty-two inches doesn't qualify as a big-screen TV because it's normal to most people. I just wanted to encourage him in his purchase.)

A few weeks after our conversation, I went to visit my dad. The first thing I did was check out his new TV. There it was, set out as a prized possession right in the middle of the living room. I turned it on expecting to share the magical moment of watching SportsCenter in HD with my dad. But as I began to flip through the channels, I noticed something curiously familiar. There were only thirteen channels, and they didn't come in clearly. You could describe the television experience as "*thirty-two* inches of haze."

Quickly, I put two and two together. My dad had gotten a new TV, but he still hadn't called the cable guy. He wasn't even planning to! We had had local stations and three religious channels growing up, and that was still all he had. He was wired for high-definition, but high-definition wasn't anywhere to be seen. We could have been watching SportsCenter in HD, but we sat there staring at haze and fuzz instead. My dad was hardwired for one thing, but he wasn't experiencing it because he hadn't called the cable guy.

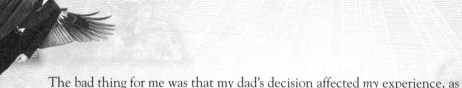

The bad thing for me was that my dad's decision affected *my* experience, as well as his.

I think this story hints at the way a lot of us experience life. We are hardwired for Eden, for utter delight, for God's best, for high-definition lives. But we're not experiencing Eden. We're stuck in the intersection between desire and tragedy. Sometimes it's because of decisions we've made, as we'll talk about tomorrow. Other times, it's because a decision that someone else made leaves consequences in our lives. Still other times, it seems almost as though evil randomly chooses us.

Mark 1:40–42 (The Voice):

Narrator: *During that time, Jesus met a man stricken with leprosy—a skin disease that many people thought made him ritually unclean.* The leper walked right up to Jesus, dropped to his knees, and begged Him for help.

Leper: If You want to, You can make me clean.

Narrator: Jesus was powerfully moved. He reached out and actually touched the leper.

Jesus: I do want to. Be clean.

Narrator: And at that very moment the disease left him; the leper was cleansed *and made whole once again.*

Naming and owning evil sometimes means naming and owning the evil that has chosen us, the evil that we've inherited. Whether it's a choice made by a parent or a loved one that has ramifications on our lives, an accident that leaves us helpless, or a life condition over which we have no control, evil can be hard to name.

But there is good news. Long before Jesus went to the cross, He cleansed people and wiped clean all of the evil that weighed them down and held them back. In this passage, Jesus was filled with compassion as He looked at a man whose life was far from what God created life to be. The Greek word translated as "powerfully moved" tells us that Jesus sighed, showing that He was deeply disturbed by what He saw. And then He acted, healing the man and changing his life forever.

While it would be wrong to use this story to say that everyone always experiences the kind of physical healing that this man did, we can at least say that Jesus cares about our suffering, that evil breaks His heart, and that He has done and will do something about it. And because He has done something about evil, He also frees us to name the goodness in our lives.

I think about it this way: the whole world breaks down into global warming and trust funds. Some of us come into life behind. We suffer consequences of choices that were made for us or made by other people, and we have to wonder what to do with the hand we've been dealt. It's like global warming in that we have to deal with a reality created by someone else's mistakes. Others of us come into life ahead. We live off the good that others have chosen for us and around us, and so we have advantages such as trust funds. The choices and decisions others have made for us have set us up for life that is better than we deserve.

Some of us inherit global warming, some of us inherit trust funds, and most of us inherit a mix of the two. The question today is not just what were you born into?—it's, what will you do with it? Trust funds can be squandered, and global warming can be reversed. So whatever you inherited, whether your story is filled with more good than evil or more evil than good, bring your story to the feet of Jesus.

by 12:28 Here's Your Challenge— Now You're on the Clock

By 12:28 tomorrow, go to the feet of Jesus. Use the story line that you created yesterday as you approach Him. At the places marked by evil, name the evil and let Jesus wipe you clean of it. At the places marked by goodness, name that goodness and thank Him for it.

DAY 3: Evil Chosen

by Chad Norris

To this day, I have no idea why I did it. Just the thought of it still makes me want me throw up. I willingly chose evil.

I grew up with a guy whom I'll call "Marty." We were great friends, but one day everything changed. I was shooting basketball with another friend when Marty came walking by. My friend and I thought it would be funny if we beat Marty up. I don't know what came over me, and even now I can't believe I did it. I remember feeling so dirty later that night—so evil. Marty and I stopped hanging out or even talking. The evil I chose shattered our friendship.

Have you ever been there? Have you ever willingly chosen evil in your own story? Yesterday, we thought about how to name and deal with evil that we've inherited in our lives. But we must be honest and admit that we will-ingly choose evil in our lives as well.

---

2 Samuel 11:1–4 (The Voice):

In the springtime of the year, the season when *most* kings took their soldiers out to fight, David stayed in Jerusalem and sent Joab out *as general* in charge of all his troops. They attacked the Ammonites and put the city of Rabbah under siege.

Early one evening, David rose from his couch and was strolling on the palace roof, when he saw a woman bathing *on a roof below.* She was very beautiful. David sent someone to find out who the woman was, and the answer came back that she was Bathsheba, the daughter of Eliam, and the wife of Uriah the Hittite. *Uriah was one of David's officers who had gone to war with the rest of David's troops.*

David *couldn't get her off his mind, so he* sent messengers to bring Bathsheba to him. She came, and they had sex. Soon after she returned home, Bathsheba realized she was pregnant, and she sent this news to David. Since their encounter occurred just after the purifying bath after her period, *her husband Uriah could not have been the father.*

One day, King David was walking around on his roof when, all of the sudden, "Holy cow!" Nobody made David choose evil. Nobody was holding a gun to his head. But David chose to lust after Bathsheba, commit adultery with her, have her husband Uriah killed, and then cover it up with a lie. David chose evil that affected his life, Bathsheba's life, Uriah's life, the life of the child that Bathsheba conceived, and then continued to ripple out.

It's scary, isn't it? It's not easy to talk about, because we all know that we have chosen evil in our lives. David isn't the only sinner in this story. And if we are to embrace the story of good in our lives, we have to own up to our own evil.

That is what I did with Marty. Fifteen years after the awful incident, I called him up and asked him to lunch. I hadn't seen him since high school. I told him I was sorry, and we both cried. Thankfully, he forgave me. Still, for the rest of my life, I will have to live with the memory of that evil.

Good stories tell of the intersection of desire and tragedy, the collision of what you wanted and what you got. Sometimes these stories have happy endings, and sometimes they don't. But our call is to address the evil we have chosen and to deal with it. It's not fun. It never will be. But we need to do this, so that the next time we think about choosing evil, we will be reminded that it's not worth it.

by 12:28 Here's Your Challenge— Now You're on the Clock

By 12:28 tomorrow, confess your choice. All of us have chosen evil. Go to God in prayer and confess the evil that you have chosen, but not yet dealt with. As you do, thank God for dealing with us mercifully when we confess to Him.

DAY 4: Dealing with Evil

by Chad Norris

"This is the year that I'm going to lose a bunch of weight."

Every January, I say the same thing. It's like a broken record. The new diet or plan or "lifestyle change" usually lasts about a month, and then I'm back to my old ways. When February comes around, my wife asks me what happened to my goal. That's the point when I come up with an excuse. I've come up with some great ones over the years, to the point that it's almost natural to create one. But the reality is that they're just excuses to cover up the fact that I haven't really dealt with my weight.

John 6:64–71 (The Voice):

Jesus: But some of you do not believe.

Narrator: From the first day *Jesus began to call disciples*, He knew those who did not have genuine faith. He knew too who would betray Him.

Jesus: This is why I have been telling you that no one comes to Me without the Father's blessing and guidance.

Narrator: After hearing these teachings, many of His disciples walked away and no longer followed Jesus.

Jesus *(to the twelve)***:** Do you want to walk away too?

Simon Peter: Lord, if we were to go, who would we follow? You speak the words that give everlasting life. We believe and recognize You as the Holy One of God.

Jesus: I chose each one of you, the twelve, Myself. But one of you is a devil.

Narrator: This cryptic comment referred to Judas the son of Simon Iscariot, for he was the one of the twelve who was going to betray Him.

In this passage, Jesus gave teachings so difficult that many followers decided to abandon Him. They just couldn't take it anymore. They made an excuse and said, "I can't do this anymore. It's just too hard."

This week, we're taking time to be really honest. All of us have evil in our lives, whether it's evil we chose or evil we inherited. The question is whether we deal with this evil by making excuses or by really dealing with it. There may be plenty of legitimate reasons for the evil in our lives, but making excuses about evil will never help us. Instead, we have to name evil and then deal with it.

If I want to lose weight, I have to be a big boy and deal with it. And if I want to deal with evil in my life, I have to own it instead of blaming everybody else. The time for excuses is over; it's time to deal with it. This may mean you go to counseling. This may mean you wrestle with evil on your own. This may mean you tell someone else of the evil you've chosen so that he or she can hold you accountable. Whatever the method is, own your evil. Deal with it. Don't make any more excuses.

by 12:2∞ Here's Your Challenge— Now You're on the Clock

By 12:28 tomorrow, excuse yourself. You've already named evil in your life this week and thought about where it came from. Today, ask God to help you evaluate what route of healing you need to pursue. Make a list below of the excuses that keep you from doing this. Then excuse yourself from these excuses and, instead, choose to take the first step toward dealing with the evil that's part of your story right now.

DAY 5: After the Ark

by Chris Brooks

The memorable melody and simple lyrics of the song "Somewhere over the Rainbow" made the song an instant classic from the moment it debuted in the movie *The Wizard of Oz* in 1939. Judy Garland's performance as "Dorothy" encapsulated our childlike desires to be in a place "where troubles melt like lemon drops." Since then, those words have been sung by artists from Diana Ross to the Smashing Pumpkins to the Veggie Tales. So it might surprise you that when MGM executives first screened *The Wizard of Oz*, someone sent out a memo that told the filmmakers, "The rainbow song is no good. Take it out." Can you imagine *The Wizard of Oz* without that Academy Award–winning song?[1]

Likewise, can you imagine what kind of story you would have if you took some of the painful and tragic chapters out of your life? We've talked this week about how good stories tell of the intersection of desire and tragedy. What makes your story and mine worth telling is that as we travel down the yellow-brick road of God's kingdom, we seek the hope, promise, and fulfillment that lie on the other side of the rainbow. This is why we have spent an entire week doing the hard work of naming evil and brokenness and starting to deal with it—so we can push through to the hope and promise of a better tomorrow.

But I must warn you that, just like the idiot who wrote the memo at MGM, not everyone will appreciate *your* song. It took me about twenty years to have enough courage to name out loud some of the tragic and shameful chapters of my story. It was gut-wrenching and humiliating to name out loud the evil that I inherited. It was even more devastating to take ownership of the evil I had freely chosen. But this was the biggest and best step I have taken in understanding the intersection of desire and tragedy in my story and God's story.

This is something you must do yourself. No one else can tell your story for you. In fact, many of us have been wounded deeply by someone who tried to help by moving us too quickly past the story of evil into the story of good. When I was growing up, I was given pat answers all the time to justify evil instead of having a safe environment where I could ask the hard questions that the story we live in demands. I see this all the time when I'm on the road speaking, and nothing angers me more than people who have not been able to name their tragedy and grieve. A fifteen-year-old boy who lost his older brother in a car accident is told that God had a plan for his brother's death because three students accepted Christ at the funeral. A mother chokes on the words "God is good" as she is told that God gave her newborn son cancer for a reason. And silent tears stream down the cheeks of sexually abused girls as they are told God is in control of everything.

I truly believe that God redeems the evil and tragic events in our lives. But often, when well-intentioned people say of a painful situation that God intended only good, grieving people hear that He directly caused evil to shatter their lives. This is a dangerous and potentially catastrophic theological statement that short-circuits the grieving process and encourages repression and outright rebellion.

Genesis 9:12–17 (The Voice):

God *(to Noah and his sons)*: Here is how I sign the *perpetual* covenant I now make with you and all the living until the end of time. I will hang a rainbow among the clouds as a signature of the covenant between Me and the earth. Whenever a cloud takes shape over the earth and a rainbow sheers the sky, I shall remember the covenant I am making with you and the living and My promise that a deluge will never again destroy the living. When I see *the beauty of* the rainbow, I will remember this covenant I have made with the living, even with the smallest living creature on earth.

    (to Noah): *Look for My rainbow, and remember My promise.* With it I sign the covenant I have made between Me and every living thing on the earth.

If God's goal was to get rid of evil with the flood, then He didn't do a very good job. Perhaps that wasn't His goal. Perhaps His goal was actually to show us how His heart breaks when evil corrupts His creation.

God does not, and will not, oversimplify the complex story of good and evil. Therefore, we must tread with great caution when we try to help others name which circumstances hold good and which hold evil in their lives. Indeed, every human endeavor is a complex mix of the two. Our calling is to name the good in our stories and carry it on, but we must also name the evil, grieve it, end its decay, and ultimately partner with God in redeeming it.

After all, the best stories are the ones where a flaw is the doorway to redemption—the stories where evil cracked through, but good used that same crack to explode in and triumph. Death and evil have been ultimately defeated, but that doesn't exclude us from experiencing death and evil now. Still, we fall forward into this story of good and evil because, at the end of the day, we trust the Author, and we trust that He will ultimately take evil and death and violence on Himself for the sake of His creation.

by 12:28 Here's Your Challenge— Now You're on the Clock

By 12:28 tomorrow, find your plot twist. Earlier this week, you drew a story arc and plotted out the landmark events of desire and tragedy in your life. Now share this story arc with someone you trust and see if together you can discover where the plot turns. Dust for God's fingerprints and see if you can discover where good is flooding back through a crack left by evil. Look for the drama of tragedy. Laugh at the irony of redemption. And live in the story of good overcoming evil.

SESSION

The Giving Tree

Look Back at the Tree That Changed Everything

Video Discussion

Look back, live forward.

Do you remember the moment when you first realized you had some filth in you? When you looked into your own eyes in the mirror and saw that there is evil in you? That moment can be one of the worst in your life. Similarly, it's shocking to realize that, although the death of loved ones is not our doing, the death of Jesus *is* something we are actually responsible for. Because we are descendants of Adam, we had something to do with the death of our King— even before we were born!

"Evil did its worst
     All the dominos crushed the cartilage
          of a dead rabbi
          Hanging from a dead tree
It was finished
It was paid for
It was Friday
     It was Friday
          It was Friday
It was Friday, but Sunday was a-comin'
And the insurrection of the
     resurrection had begun

Tick tock, tick tock
Death had begun to die
Tick tock, tick tock
     Redemption is rolling up its sleeves
          and taking off its tie
Tick tock, tick tock
Spring has sprung
And from out of Eden's twilight
     Here comes our cry:
     "EVIL, let us LIVE!"

Because all in all
You're just another brick in the wall
     That is cracked
          And crumbling
               And decaying
Every time the church is
          saying,
     "Christ is crucified"
     "Christ is risen"
     And "Christ is coming"
Again and again and
          again and again
We sing it
     We preach it
          We dance it
               We whisper it to
                    ourselves
                    . . . Twice daily."

Isaiah 53:4–7
(The Voice)

So He was dismissed *at best*
And sometimes abused. We
   didn't think much of Him,
This man of constant suffering,
   grief's patient friend. . . .
He kept a low profile.
We simply didn't notice Him
   most of the time.
Yet *(so small a word for such*
   terrible truth)
It was our suffering He carried,
   our pain
And distress, our sick-to-the-
   soul-ness. . . .
He endured the breaking that
   made us whole.
His injuries became our
   healing.

The truth is, we are guilty. We are responsible for Jesus' death. But Satan is trying to deceive us about the Cross. He sits on the back row of churches, convincing us to pray prayers that are future-oriented rather than embrace the forgiveness that we *already* have been given. For those of us who are in Christ Jesus, the freedom we long for has *already* been purchased. We have *already* received it. We *have* the freedom to live! If evil is dominating your life, look back, live forward.

Jesus is described as "grief's patient friend." How does it make you feel to know that Jesus suffered to make you free?

How is your pain affected by the Cross?

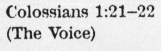

Colossians 1:21–22 (The Voice)

You were once at odds *with God*, wicked in your ways and evil in your minds, but now the Liberating King has reconciled you by His body—in His flesh, through His death—that you would be presentable to God, holy, blameless, and totally free of sin and guilt.

Martin Luther had an encounter with the Word of God that changed his mind. He found that the Bible told him he was clean and forgiven here and now, not just one day far off in the future in heaven. So Luther began to teach this message to his students, and he told them of the importance of preaching the gospel to yourself every day.

Many of us would think this means asking, "Do I know that I know that I know that I *know* I'm going to heaven when I die?" But the Cross is not a one-stop shop to get to heaven. The message of the gospel story is not "here's how to get to heaven," but "here's how to truly have a relationship with God." Why wait until heaven to know and love Jesus?

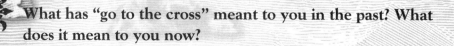 **What has "go to the cross" meant to you in the past? What does it mean to you now?**

Romans 5:18–19 (The Voice)

So here is the result: as one man's sin brought about condemnation *and punishment* for all people, so one man's act of faithfulness makes all of us right with God and brings us to new life. Just as through one man's *defiant* disobedience all of us were made sinners, so through the *humble* obedience of the one man every one of us will be made right.

Chad tells the story of dancing for his daughter, Ruthie, every night before she goes to bed. It took her six months, but one night her little shoulders started swaying, and she joined in the dance. God's waiting for you to join His dance, too. Today and every day, God is inviting you to embrace Him and to experience a love story that He made possible through Jesus' suffering. Will you get out on the floor?

How has God danced for you in your life, and how do you
join Him in the jig?

How do you want God to see you?

Daily Readings

DAY 1: Come to the Cross

by Chad Norris

I don't have many chores at my house. The boss lady (a.k.a. my wife) expects me to do only a couple of things: feed the kids in the morning and take out the trash once a week. That's it. But I have to be honest, I hate taking out the trash every single Thursday over and over and over. I would rather be beaten in the face with a boat paddle than take out the trash. I wish I could take it out just once a year and be done with it—or maybe even just once in a lifetime. I just get sick of taking out the trash!

Colossians 1:21–22 (The Voice):

You were once at odds *with God,* wicked in your ways and evil in your minds, but now the Liberating King has reconciled you by His body—in His flesh through His death—that you would be presentable to God, holy, blameless, and totally free of sin and guilt.

Martin Luther is one of the most prominent figures in church history. But before he began the Reformation, he was tortured because he had a false view of God. He was convinced that God hated him. He felt condemned and unholy most of the time. I think many of us can relate.

But Luther had an encounter with the Word of God that changed his mind. He found that the Bible told him that he was clean and forgiven here and now, not just one day in heaven. He read passages like the one we're looking at today in Colossians. So Luther began to preach what he had learned to his students, and he told them of the importance of preaching the gospel to yourself every day.

If Martin Luther had to preach the gospel to himself every day, then I need to do it as well. Even more frequently than I have to take out the trash, I need to come to the cross, reminding myself of how God stepped into my story to break the cycle of evil and once again start a story of good. I am clean because of the blood of Christ—not just clean one day in heaven, but clean here and now.

If you and I don't go to the cross to get this truth into our hearts every day, we won't be able to live out this reality. We look back to live forward.

Here's Your Challenge— Now You're on the Clock

By 12:28 tomorrow, preach to yourself. Find a verse of Scripture to meditate on and memorize, such as today's passage or Romans 8:1. Say the verse out loud several times slowly to begin to get it into your mind. Then the next time you do a chore, like taking out the trash, take a moment to preach to yourself by saying this verse out loud. Let this verse help you continually look back to the cross, so that you can live forward.

DAY 2: He Died for Our Iniquities

by Dave Rhodes

I'm not a big beach guy (which is odd for someone who spent so much of his life in Florida). I'm just not a fan of hot sand, and I've seen *Jaws* a few too many times to get pumped up about swimming in the ocean. I know it's just a movie, but somehow I can almost hear the *Jaws* theme music as soon as I step foot in the water. So on most days I prefer the pool to the beach.

But whenever I get the chance to go snorkeling out in the deep water, I get caught between desire and fear. I love watching the beautiful fish and sea life. I love getting lost in the world beneath the water. I just wish all that stuff was in the pool! When I'm in the ocean, snorkeling, my head is constantly on a swivel as I try to make sure that I see Jaws in enough time to be the one guy who gets out of the water right before the shark starts eating people. However, the past few times I've gone snorkeling, it wasn't the sharks that posed the biggest threat—it was the barracudas.

Last summer, I went snorkeling in Key Largo. I got into the water, and there he was—a four-foot barracuda staring me right in the face in a way that only a barracuda can. His mysterious glare went right through me in a way that made me want to start confessing my deepest sins and insecurities. His razor-sharp teeth peeking out of his slightly opened mouth hinted at the damage he could do to me if he wanted to. The way he just seemed to hover over me haunted me in the deepest recesses of my soul.

I almost got out of the water, but on this particular snorkeling trip, there was something in the water I really wanted to see: Jesus. I'm not joking, and this isn't a metaphor. Jesus was really in the water. Well, at least an eight-and-a-half-foot statue of Him was. They call it *Jesus of the Abyss*. This four-thousand-pound bronze statue depicting Jesus with His arms spread wide stands twenty-five feet under water. This statue, which was made from the same cast as a statue that lies off the coast of Italy, was given to the Underwater Society of America and placed in the waters off Key Largo in 1965. Now people from all over the world go there to snorkel and see the statue. So there I was, wanting to see Jesus, but finding a four-foot barracuda obstructing my way.

That's the way it always is with Jesus, isn't it? You really want to get to Him, but there's a barracuda that keeps you away. Sometimes having to stare at our own sin and evil keeps us from Jesus, because it's frightening to be in the water with that kind of barracuda.

Isaiah 6:1–7 (The Voice):

Narrator: In the same year that the king *here in Judah*, Uzziah, died, *I received a vision.* I saw the Lord sitting on a grand throne way up high with a flowing cape that filled the whole temple. *Bright flaming creatures,* seraphs *as they are known,* waited on Him. Each had six wings: two covering its face *out of respect for God's glory,* two covering its feet, and two for flying. *Like some fiery choir,* they would call back and forth continually.

Seraphs: Holy, holy, holy! The Eternal One *is holy.* Holy is the Commander of heaven's forces! And the earth is filled with His beauty and glory!

Narrator: They were so loud that the doorframes shook, and the holy house kept filling with smoke.

Isaiah: I am in so much trouble! *I shouldn't be here!* I'm just a human being, fallible and stammering, and I live with people faulted like me. But *here I am, and* I've seen with my very own eyes *none other than* the King, the Commander of heaven's forces, the Eternal One.

Narrator: Then one of the flaming creatures flew to me holding a red-hot ember, which it had taken from *God's table,* the temple altar, with a pair of tongs. The creature held it to my lips.

Seraph: With the touch of this burning ember on your lips, your guilt will turn away; all your faults and wrongdoings will be absolved.

Isaiah came to see God, but when God showed up, so did the barracuda of Isaiah's own sin and evil. And before Isaiah could be made clean of all that stuff, he had to own his sin and evil. He had to humble himself and bring that stuff to God. It is with this confession that Isaiah began his journey toward freedom.

I think the same is true for us. It's easy to talk about evil and sin as someone else's problem—but Jesus offers us a different alternative. He invites us into the abyss with Him. He wants us to dive down and find that the Cross really is enough. We have to look back at the Cross, an event that happened thousands of years ago, so that we can live forward here and now. By looking back at the Cross, we find healing for the sin and evil we have chosen—for our iniquities—and we find freedom to live the life that God intends for us.

by 12:28 Here's Your Challenge— Now You're on the Clock

By 12:28 tomorrow, dive in. Find a physical depiction or an artistic representation of the cross to reflect on. As you do, take some time to meditate on the work that Christ did on the cross. Remember that on the cross, He died for all the sin and evil you have chosen. Dive into the abyss with Him and face your barracuda, trusting that His arms are spread wide for you.

DAY 3: He Died for Our Infirmities

by Dave Rhodes

This week we're talking about the Cross. We have tried to look back at what happened on the cross two thousand years ago so that we can find freedom to live forward in our lives today. We have faced the barracuda of our evil and sin and plunged into the abyss to find Jesus with His arms open wide.

But today, we go to the cross with something that might be even harder to face. We know that when we go to the cross, we need to own the evil and sin we have chosen. It's often harder, though, to go to the cross with the evil and sin that has chosen us. This is the evil we have to deal with on a regular basis because of someone else's bad choices or because of the hard stuff that happens almost at random, exposing how vulnerable we are from living in a broken world.

We know that we should go to the cross for the hurts we have given others, but we're not always sure we should bring the hurts others have given us. We know we need to go to the cross for dishonoring and rebelling against our parents, but we're not sure how to go to the cross with our parents' divorce. We know we should go to the cross when we cause bad things to happen to other people, but what happens when bad stuff happens to us? What does the Cross have to say about a hurricane in New Orleans, genocide in Darfur, or a knee injury that ends a young athlete's dream? Today we go to the cross with *this* kind of evil, these infirmities in our lives.

Romans 5:14–21 (The Voice):

Still, death plagued all humanity from Adam to Moses, even those whose sin was of a different sort than Adam's. *You see, in God's plan* Adam was a prototype of the One who comes *to usher in a new day.* But the free gift of grace bears no resemblance to Adam's crime *that brings a death sentence to all of humanity; in fact, it is quite the opposite.* For if the one man's sin brings death to so many, how much more does the gift of God's *radical* grace extend to humanity, since the One—Jesus the Liberating King—offered His generous gift. His free gift is nothing like *the scourge of* the first man's sin. For the judgment that fell because of one false step brought condemnation, but the free gift following countless offenses results in a favorable verdict. If one man's sin brought a reign of death—*that's Adam's legacy*—how much more will those who receive grace in abundance and the free gift of righteousness reign in life by means of one other man—Jesus the Liberating King.

So here is the result: as one man's sin brought about condemnation *and punishment* for all people, so one man's act of faithfulness makes all of us right with God and brings us to new life. Just as through one man's *defiant* disobedience every one of us were made sinners, so through the *humble* obedience of the one man every one of us will be made right.

When the law came into the picture, sin grew and grew, but where sin has spread, grace is there to cut it down and defeat it. *No matter how much sin crept in, there was always more grace.* In the same way that sin has reigned in the sphere of death, now grace reigns through God's righteousness *eclipsing death* and leading to eternal life through Jesus the Liberating King, our Lord.

The Cross reverses the dominos that Adam and Eve flipped in Genesis 3. Yes, evil and sin are always present in our broken, fallen world. But God has stepped into this story of brokenness to begin writing a new story of redemption. It's a story of love and hope and new life. It takes place right in the middle of the greatest brokenness, at ground zero, and it points to the possibility of a new future.

A couple of years ago, I was doing a retreat in Oklahoma City, and I had a couple of extra hours to burn before my flight home. Because I don't really enjoy spending extended time in unfamiliar airports, I was looking for something else to pass the time. So when the Oklahoma scenery—which seems to be the same two miles repeated over and over again—was broken up with signs advertising a memorial downtown, it caught my attention. I remembered seeing the horrific Oklahoma City bombing on TV when I was in college, and I thought that I would pull into the memorial to see firsthand the recounting of this awful event. I wasn't prepared for what I saw and heard.

April 19, 1995, started out like pretty much every other day. In a way eerily similar to the beautiful New York morning of September 11, 2001, the day began with clear skies. At 9:01 AM everything was normal. By 9:03 the entire world had changed, because at 9:02 a bomb went off outside the Murrah Federal Building, destroying the facility and killing 168 people. I watched in horror as I made my way through the retelling of these events. Sometimes, you're just not prepared for evil to be displayed undisguised. Brokenness, death, and suffering seemed to rule that day.

But as I made my way through the memorial, another story began to emerge from the ashes. It was a story of hope and redemption—a story of people standing in lines to donate blood, of firemen and police making daring rescues, and of ordinary people opening their homes in extraordinary ways. This story assured me that evil does not always have the last word.

I stepped outside the memorial and noticed a field full of 168 chairs, which represented the people who died that dreadful day. Markers on each side of the monument read 9:01 and 9:03 to frame that fateful moment. And then, as I turned to leave, I noticed a tree in the middle of the memorial. It's known as the Survivor Tree. This elm tree, which is at least one hundred years old and stood in a parking lot opposite the Murrah Federal Building when the blast struck, weathered the explosion. In a parking lot where cars were upended and pavement was blown to shreds, this tree held strong. The survivors of that awful day saw hope in this tree, which now stands in this memorial and bears the slogan: "The spirit of this city and this nation will not be defeated; our deeply rooted faith sustains us." At ground zero, hope grows in this Survivor Tree.

The story of the Cross tells us of another survivor tree. On this tree, the King of the universe died for all of our iniquities and all of our infirmities. He died for the evil we chose and the evil that chose us. He took all that evil onto Himself so that at ground zero we can have hope—hope that the new story of redemption will have its say in our individual stories.

I don't know what evil you are dealing with today, and I don't know what questions you have about the suffering you see in the world. I probably have similar questions. But I know that a tree grows at ground zero and that at this tree we all find hope for our future.

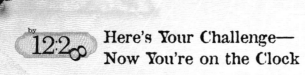

Here's Your Challenge—
Now You're on the Clock

by 12:28

By 12:28 tomorrow, go to ground zero. Use the Internet to do some research on some of the suffering that's going on in the world. Look honestly at poverty. Stare into the eyes of those who have been devastated by tragedy. See your own tragedy through their eyes and bring all of it to the cross. Then let the cross be planted at your ground zero as you allow Jesus to flip back the dominos of our broken world with His new story of redemption. Determine that you will become part of His story of hope.

DAY 4: Crucified with Christ

by Chris Brooks

The idea of looking back to live forward is a powerful statement for our lives. To this point in the *Domino Effect*, we've looked back at the story of good and evil through the creation narrative and through our stories as well. As I continue to look back and try to live forward in my life, one verse galvanizes my identity in Christ, even in the face of the barracudas of my insecurities and inadequacies.

Galatians 2:20 (The Voice):

I have been crucified with the Liberating King—I am no longer alive—but the Liberator is living in me, and whatever life I have left in this failing body I have because of the faithfulness of God's Son, the One who loved me and gave Himself *on the cross* for me.

Don't you love it? In the eyes of God, you have been crucified with Christ. Your iniquities, your infirmities, your old identity, the evil you chose, and the evil that chose you—all of it is crucified with Christ! I want to turn this verse into a heart-thumping, jaw-dropping rock anthem so that we can all scream at the top of our lungs and light our Zippos every time we are tempted to look back at our past and wallow in fear or shame or the lie that God doesn't like us very much. According to this verse, when God sees those of us who are in Christ Jesus, He sees us through His Son. Jesus, part of the triune God, has adopted us into Sonship and offered His righteousness, His acceptance, and identity in Him.

If you spend any time reading what I've written or listening to what I've said, you will soon realize that I have an unhealthy obsession with English bulldogs. I know they're fat, ugly, lazy, and messy, and they smell like nuclear waste, but I still love them and think they are irresistible. Secretly, I pray this is how God sees me—minus the shedding and licking, of course.

Albus was my first English bulldog. He was a wreck, but he was mine. His identity was "my bulldog, Albus." Was he "my bulldog, Albus" when he

had been perfect all day and was patiently sitting, waiting for me to pet him and play with him when I got home? Yes. Was he still "my bulldog, Albus" on the days when I came home and he had desecrated our carpet, chewed up the leg of our kitchen table, and tried to tackle me when I walked in the door? Yes. He was still "my bulldog, Albus," because his identity was not determined by his behavior—it was determined by my love for him and the price I paid for that love.

When Albus was just a puppy, I went to a breeder and paid way too much money for the right to point my finger at a litter of puppies and say, "That one is mine." From that moment on, I could always look back and say that no matter what happened, that puppy was "my bulldog, Albus."

In an even more profound way, God has pointed to each of us and said, "That one is mine." From the moment we accept this, we live in the reality of being crucified with Christ, and nothing can change our identity as His children. So we can look back at the cross and live in response to what happened on it. At the cross, the price of evil was paid in full. The glorious message of the cross is that the domino effect is reversed and evil no longer has the final say in our lives, in our relationships, and most importantly, in our identity.

by 12:28 Here's Your Challenge— Now You're on the Clock

By 12:28 tomorrow, just breathe. Inhale God and exhale your identity. When you inhale, say the word *Abba*, which is the Hebrew word for "Father" that Jesus used for God. When you exhale, say, "I belong to you." Consciously and consistently do this throughout the day. As you do, intentionally remind yourself of how God sees you and how you should see yourself.

DAY 5: Look Back to Live Forward

by Chad Norris

My friend Dave Rhodes, whom you've met earlier in this series, is secretly the fastest driver on earth. He may deny this, but it's true. He drives fast and has been known to make a five-hour drive in about three hours.

One day Rhodes and I were driving from Alabama to South Carolina in two separate minivans. A group of us had been to a funeral, and we were now making the long trip back. You know that guys can get competitive, so before long these two minivans full of spouses and kids became racing machines in a quest to see who could get home the quickest.

I got a good lead on Rhodes because he had to stop for gas. Over the next four hours, I drove at breakneck speed while looking in the rearview mirror every ten seconds. I was moving forward, but much of my focus was on a minivan behind me. I was looking back as I tried to live forward. (For the record, my wife had to make a restroom stop, and I lost the race. I'm still not over it. I guess Rhodes isn't the only competitive person I know.)

---

1 Peter 2:24–25 (The Voice):

He took on our sins in his body when He died on the cross so that we, being dead to sin, can live for righteousness. *As the Scripture says,* "through His wounds, you were healed." For there was a time when you were like wandering sheep, but now you have returned to the Shepherd and Guardian of your lives.

We often make a huge mistake when it comes to following Christ by waiting for God to do something in our future. Now, this is not sin, and obviously we ought to hope for God to work in our lives and situations. But something has *already* happened to change us.

Think about it this way: Has Jesus died on the cross, or is He going to die on the cross in the *future?* Obviously, He has already died. It's past tense. Has Jesus healed us by His wounds, or is He going to heal us in the *future?* As Peter wrote, we are *already* healed. Because of the blood that has *already*

been shed, we can be healed and whole *here and now*. Maybe the reason we struggle to live forward is that we never look back in our rearview mirror.

We should live forward while keeping our eyes on what happened on the cross. The Cross makes us whole. It has already happened. Turn around and look at it, and then use the Cross to move forward. When we do this, we live as disciples who are always aware of what our King has done for us. So take a peek.

by 12:28 Here's Your Challenge— Now You're on the Clock

By 12:28 tomorrow, look in the rearview mirror. Read this week's passage, Isaiah 53, slowly and deliberately. As you do this, remind yourself that all this has already happened. Thank Jesus for what He did on the cross to allow us to live forward.

SESSION

View of a Branch

Curse the Tree Where Neutral Is Normal

Video Discussion

No good is not good, and not good is evil.

For many a kid at summer camp, free time at the pool is well spent waiting in line for even one jump from the high board. You have options up there—to be the "big-splash guy," the "great-dive guy," or the "belly-flop guy." And the competition can get fierce in the battle to impress at the high-board showdown. But if fear takes over and refuses to allow your body to act, you end up going off the board in the classic jump known as the "pencil."

"But we still, still have a fig tree
    with no figs
A temple with no tact
A religion with no regard
And a bunch of services, but no
    servants
    Willing to take care of the
        widow, the orphan, and
        the foreigner

So Jesus said in the King James
    Version,
"Bump dat and flip dat house
Upside down and inside out"
Forcing us to see
That sometimes
The way up is to go down
And sometimes
The way to grasp your life
Is to let go of it."

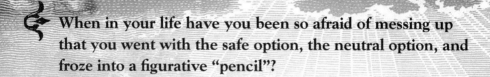

 When in your life have you been so afraid of messing up that you went with the safe option, the neutral option, and froze into a figurative "pencil"?

Pretty much everyone has a problem with the evil out there in the world. We have a strong dislike for people and things that are destructive, such as terrorism, genocide, and oppression. But we have a hard time seeing that when we do nothing, we contribute to the story of evil in the world, too.

 How does doing nothing contribute to the story of evil? Is it fair to compare it to terrorism, genocide, or oppression?

 Do you go to the cross for freedom from your own personal evil only, or do you also go for the freedom of the world?

Mark 11:12–25 (The Voice):

Narrator: The next morning, when they departed Bethany and were traveling back to the city, Jesus was hungry. Off in the distance, He saw a fig tree fully leafed out, so He headed toward it to see if it might have any ripe fruit. But when He reached it, He found only leaves because the fig season had not yet come.

As the disciples listened, *Jesus pronounced a curse on the tree.*

Jesus: No one will ever eat fruit from your branches again.

Narrator: They continued into Jerusalem *and made their way up to the temple.*

Upon reaching the temple *that morning,* Jesus dealt with those who were selling and buying *animals for sacrifices* and drove them out of the area. He turned over the tables of those who exchanged money *for the temple pilgrims* and the seats of those selling birds, and He *physically* prevented anyone from carrying anything through the temple.

Jesus *(to those who were listening)***:** Didn't the prophets write, "My house will be called a house of prayer, for all the people," but you have made it into a "haven for thieves"?

Narrator: The chief priests and the scribes heard these words *and knew Jesus was referring to them,* so they plotted His destruction. They had grown afraid of Him because His teachings struck the crowds into astonishment.

When evening came, Jesus [and His followers] left the city again. The next morning *on the way back to Jerusalem,* they passed a tree that had withered down to its very roots.

Peter *(remembering)***:** That's the fig tree, Teacher, the one You cursed *just yesterday morning.* It's withered away *to nothing!*

Jesus: Trust in God. *If you do,* honestly, you can say to this mountain, "Mountain, uproot yourself and throw yourself into the sea." If you don't doubt, but trust that what you say will take place, then it will happen. So listen to what I'm saying: Whatever you pray for or ask *from God,* believe that you'll receive it and you will. When you pray, if you remember anyone who has wronged you, forgive him so that God above can also forgive you.

In this passage, Jesus encounters a fig tree that does not bear fruit. Jesus' response is not simple frustration, the way you might feel at the end of a long day if you found in your freezer an empty carton of your favorite ice cream. Jesus' reaction—strong and instant—speaks to a greater theme in the story. The fig tree represents the nation of Israel, the way an eagle is symbolic of the United States or a palmetto tree the state of South Carolina. So when Jesus saw that fruitless tree, He saw an entire nation of people who were refusing to worship God as they should—a mistake they had made continually throughout their history.

 In what ways are Christians like fig trees without figs? In what ways are you?

Christians should be known more for doing good than for opposing evil. It's great to stand up for God, but if we are not emulating Christ in grace *and* in truth as we do this, we could obstruct someone's view of the cross. If we are going to live with the name of Christ, our goal should be to present a real picture of Christ to the people around us, so that people will want to know *more* about Christ because of us, not *less*.

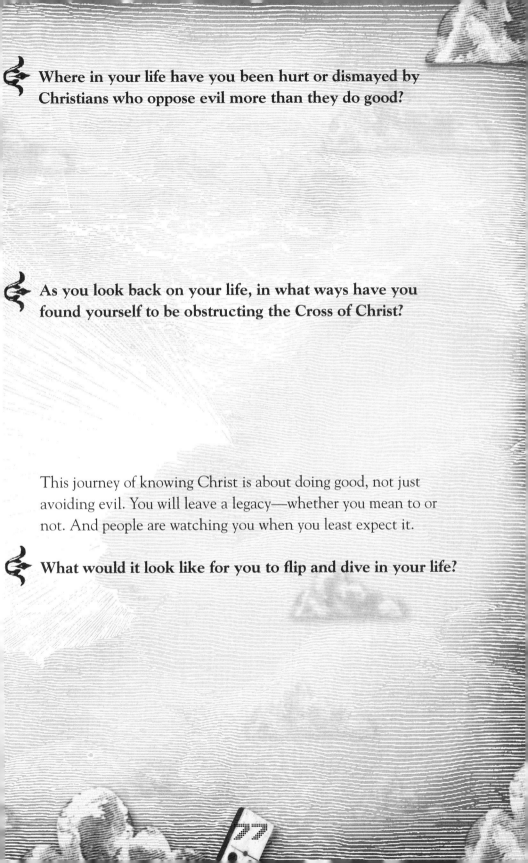

Where in your life have you been hurt or dismayed by Christians who oppose evil more than they do good?

As you look back on your life, in what ways have you found yourself to be obstructing the Cross of Christ?

This journey of knowing Christ is about doing good, not just avoiding evil. You will leave a legacy—whether you mean to or not. And people are watching you when you least expect it.

What would it look like for you to flip and dive in your life?

DAY 1: No Such Thing as Neutral

by Dave Rhodes

Imagine this: You're so thirsty that your tongue seems to be stuck to the roof of your mouth. You have a hard time swallowing because of the cotton-mouth feeling that has overwhelmed you. You need liquid, and you need it now. Then out of the corner of your eye, you see it. It's liquid hope for your desperation. At first, you think it might be a mirage, but as you get closer, you realize that your eyes have not deceived you. It's a drink machine! What could taste better than an ice-cold drink? The promise seems so real that you can almost taste it.

So you quickly dig into your pocket to find a dollar and a quarter to put in the machine. But the machine won't take your dollar bill. You go through the arduous task of smoothing out your bill time and time again, but it continues to be rejected. Finally, on the fifth try, the dollar bill is accepted. You drop in the quarter and push the button to release the liquid gold. But what happens? *Nothing.* You push the button again and again. *Nothing.* You shake the machine and again—*nothing.* Now you try to push the button to get your money back, but still, *nothing* happens. You kick the machine and curse at it, as it stares back at you with *nothing.* In a cruel twist of irony, the refrigerator generator kicks on to let you know the drinks locked inside this machine are being chilled to perfection. Now you're even thirstier, and you're angry, too.

Does this sound familiar to you? We've probably all been held captive by a vending machine at one time or another. In fact, even now I can feel the frustration of my worst vending-machine nightmares. There's nothing worse than a vending machine that's out of order—except for a vending machine that's out of order with no sign warning you of this! This fraud of a machine raises your expectations only to let you down by doing *nothing.*

Matthew 25:14–30 (The Voice):

Bridegroom: *This is how it will be.* It will be like a landowner who is going on a trip. He instructed his slaves about caring for his property. He gave five talents to one slave, two to the next, and then one talent to the last slave—each according to his ability. Then the man left.

Narrator: Promptly the man who had been given five talents went out and bartered and sold and turned his five talents into ten. And the one who had received two talents *went to the market and* turned his two into four. And the slave who had received just one talent? He dug a hole in the ground and buried his master's money there.

Eventually, the master came back from his travels, *found his slaves,* and settled up with them. The slave who had been given five talents came forward and told his master how he'd turned five into ten; *then he handed the whole lot over to his master.*

Master: Excellent. *You've proved yourself not only clever, but loyal.* You've executed a rather small task masterfully, so now I am going to put you in charge of something larger. *But before you go back to work,* come join my great feast and celebration.

Narrator: Then the slave who had been given two talents came forward and told his master how he'd turned two into four, *and he handed all four talents to his master.*

Master: Excellent. *You've proved yourself not only clever, but loyal.* You've executed a rather small task masterfully, so now I am going to put you in charge of something larger. *But before you go back to work,* come join my great feast and celebration.

Narrator: Finally, the man who had been given one talent came forward.

Servant: Master, I know you are a hard man, *difficult in every way. You can make a healthy sum when others would fail.* You profit when other people are doing the work. You grow rich on the backs of others. So I was afraid, *dug a hole,* and hid the talent in the ground. Here it is. You can have it.

Narrator: *The master was furious.*

Master: You are a pathetic excuse for a servant! *You have disproved my trust in you and squandered my generosity. It would be better for you if you were utterly ignorant, but you don't have that excuse.* You know I am interested in making profit! You could have at least put this talent in the bank—then I could have earned a little interest on it! Take that one talent away, and give it to the servant who doubled my money from five to ten.

Narrator: You see, everything was taken away from the man who had nothing, but the man who had something got even more. *And as for the slave who had buried his talent in the ground?* His master ordered his slaves to tie him up and throw him outside into the utter darkness where there is miserable mourning and great fear.

The difficulty with this great story that Jesus told many years ago is that the villain looks so normal. He doesn't look like a character Jack Nicholson would play. Instead, he looks a lot like us. He wasn't doing anything that seems really awful—he just wasn't doing anything. But in Jesus' story, this guy was considered evil.

We can learn a lot from this story. Sometimes, the greatest evil we do as Christians is in the good we leave undone. Jesus challenges our idea of good and evil by challenging our neutrality. For Jesus, neutral is no longer neutral—it's evil. When we as Christians come to the cross for our own evil but do *nothing* for the problem of evil in the world, we find ourselves standing in the way of the cross. We become a barrier, or an obstruction, to people who are trying to deal with the story of evil in their lives.

The great tragedy isn't just that we hide our one talent in the ground but that many of us are hiding our two talents or even five talents in the ground. Too often we're living in neutral and contributing to the story of evil in the world by doing *nothing*, not realizing that no good is not good and not good is evil.

by 12:28 Here's Your Challenge— Now You're on the Clock

By 12:28 tomorrow, stop doing nothing. Find one place that you can do something for the cause of good in the world and do it. It can be as simple as writing an encouraging note to someone or as radical as signing up for a mission trip to help people in need. Just do something so that you are no longer in neutral, doing nothing.

DAY 2: Standing in the Way by Standing Still

by Chris Brooks

Imagine you are in your office working. Everyone else in your department is out at lunch except for one other workaholic who, like you, finds himself incapable of finding time to eat and work in the same day. Suddenly, you hear a loud thump and muffled groans from outside your office door. Through the window you see your co-worker experiencing what appears to be an epileptic seizure. What would you do?

If you knew you were this guy's only hope, I would guess you'd be like the 85 percent of people who would rush out and assist this person. But if a study that two New York City psychologists did is accurate, only 35 percent of you would respond to this situation if you thought someone else heard it as well. This seems counterintuitive, but this conundrum known as "the bystander problem" shows that when people are in a group, the responsibility to act is diffused. These researchers did a similar experiment with smoke coming out of someone's door. Seventy-five percent of observers reported the smoke if they were alone, but only 38 percent reported it if they were in a group.[1]

I fall into this bystander problem as a Christian. Every time I see evil or brokenness, I think that someone else will fix it. But if no good is not good and not good is evil, then for those of us who follow Christ, there is no such thing as an innocent bystander.

Mark 3:1–6 (The Voice):

Narrator: *Soon, the Pharisees had another chance to confront Jesus. On the Sabbath,* Jesus had come into a synagogue where He saw a man with a withered hand.

The Pharisees held their breath: would Jesus cure this man on the Sabbath, right there in front of everyone? If so, they could charge Him with breaking the Sabbath law. Jesus knew their hearts. He called to the man with the withered hand.

Jesus: Come to Me.

Narrator: Then He turned to the Pharisees with a question.

Jesus: Do our laws tell us to do good or evil on the Sabbath? To save life, or to snuff it out?

Narrator: They remained silent.

Jesus was furious as He looked out over the crowd, and He was grieved by their hard hearts. *How could anyone care so much about the words of the law and so little about the spirit of it?*

Jesus (*to the man with the withered hand*): *So be it.* Stretch out your hand.

Narrator: The man stretched forth his hand; and as he did, it was completely healed. The Pharisees *didn't say anything to Jesus, but their actions spoke loudly. They* went directly from the synagogue to consult with the supporters of Herod, *the Roman's puppet ruler,* about how they could get rid of this dangerous dreamer.

In this passage, Jesus launched a direct assault on what the Pharisees (and I) thought it meant to be religious. The Pharisees were convinced of their status as the religious elite, because they strictly avoided evil and sin. For the longest time, I thought I should measure spiritual maturity like the Pharisees did, based on what evil I avoided. As a student, I thought if I avoided underage drinking, premarital sex, and tobacco products, then I was more religious and spiritually mature than other people. As a young adult, I thought if I didn't cheat on my taxes, avoided drinking in excess, and abstained from premarital sex, then I was more religious and spiritually mature than other people. And now that I have a wife and kids, I sometimes think that if I don't skip out on my tithe, avoid beating my children, and abstain from extramarital sex, then I am more religious and spiritually mature than other people.

But in this passage, Jesus told the Pharisees—and tells us—that our identity as God-followers is rooted more in what we do than in what we don't do. Jesus isn't looking for neutrality, innocent bystanders, or avoiders of evil. He doesn't just want someone who is devoid of evil—He wants someone who is filled with goodness and grace, someone who is taking part in the healing and restoration of His creation and His created.

It's easy for us to be overwhelmed by the problem of evil and the weight of the needs all around us. We can even justify our neutrality by saying that we're not "called" to a specific problem or situation. But the need *is* the call. So avoiding evil is not enough. God doesn't want His followers to be known more for what they are *against* than what they are *for*. There is so much more to the story of the gospel than that. Instead of standing in the way of the cross by standing still as innocent bystanders, God wants us to be do-gooders who join Him in the story He is writing.

 What does it look like, in a day-to-day sense, to be "filled with goodness and grace," rather than simply being "devoid of evil"?

 What would it take for you to become known more for the good you do than for the evil you avoid?

Here's Your Challenge—
Now You're on the Clock

By 12:28 tomorrow, stop being a bystander. Yesterday we talked about the need to do something instead of being neutral. Today, create the opportunity to respond to the needs you come across by cutting out one bystander activity. Turn off the radio or the TV or your iPod or your computer, so you can stop and listen and look for ways to step out of the quagmire of neutrality into the rushing river of life. When you see a need, react as a do-gooder instead of as a bystander.

DAY 3: Standing in the Way by Taking the Wrong Stand

by Chad Norris

I was fifteen years old, and one of my friends was irate. He looked at me and said, "We need to go boycott the mall." I didn't know what a boycott was—I figured it might be something a Boy Scout slept on in the woods or something. My buddy was a regular at our church and a passionate follower of God, and he believed that our hometown mall stood for some wrong things. I don't remember what those things were; I just remember that this guy thought God wanted a group of fifteen-year-olds to picket the mall. I felt a lot of tension because I didn't want to go, but I thought God hated me for thinking this. Eventually, I decided to risk God's wrath and boycott the boycott.

Now, years later, I look back at my friend's boycott and smile. His passion was commendable, but somewhere along the way he decided that if you love God, you have to do something like picket a mall.

Many of us have been through this. We love God and want to serve Him, but a wrong picture of God or some bad theology tells us that we have to bash the world and embarrass the people we disagree with. It's no good, and it's not good for the message of Christ.

The truth is that we can stand in the way of the cross by taking the wrong stand. When Jesus made His stands, He usually stood against the religious establishment of His day—not those who were taking part in worldly sin. He loved people—even sinful people—in ways we cannot comprehend. The stands He took were not the stands we so often see Christians in our world taking.

---

1 Corinthians 13:1–3 (The Voice):

What if I speak as one of *the most persuasive of* people or *under the divine influence of* heavenly messengers, but live without love? Well, then, anything I say sounds like the clanging of brass or a crashing cymbal. What if I have the gift of prophecy, am blessed with knowledge and insight to all the mysteries, or what if my faith is strong enough to scoop a mountain *from its bedrock,* yet I live without love? If so, I am nothing. I could give all that I have to feed the poor, I could surrender my body to be burned *as a martyr,* but if I do not live in love, it amounts to nothing.

It's wonderful to take a stand for Christ. I think God is proud of us when we do—as long as we are imitating Him. But many people who take a stand for Christ have gotten misdirected in their passion, and this can get them into real trouble. As Paul said in this passage, we need to act out of love. This, unfortunately, is left out of many of the stands Christians take.

I know of a church that is doing everything it can in court to keep a restaurant with a bar from opening near its property. I wonder if this church ever considered having people from their church work in or eat at this restaurant so they can share the love of Christ there. Some years ago, a group of Christians decided to boycott Walt Disney World. But maybe, instead of boycotting, we should go there and live out the love of Christ in the way we talk and act.

It's not wrong to take a stand, but before we do we need to make sure we're making the right stands and doing so with the right posture. Like Paul said, love should be the centerpiece of every stand we take so that we don't stand in the way of the cross for other people.

by 12:2₀₀ Here's Your Challenge— Now You're on the Clock

By 12:28 tomorrow, stand down. Think about a stand you have taken in the past or are taking right now. Did you take that stand with love? Did you in any way stand in the way of the cross as you took that stand? Ask God to help you answer these questions honestly, and then stand down if God leads you to do so.

DAY 4: From Standing Still to Turning Back

by Chad Norris

When I was a teenager, I had a buddy whom I really wanted to lead to Christ. I never was forceful about it, and even though he wasn't a believer, we still had a great relationship through athletics and school. I hung out with this guy for several years, but I never saw him come to Christ.

One day we were having a conversation, and it suddenly became obvious to me what was keeping him from giving his life to Jesus. He brought up the name of another of our friends who was a "Christian" but did everything a non-Christian would do. Basically, this other guy, and people like him, were a huge reason that my buddy would not give his life to Christ. He was thinking, "Why should it matter if I become a Christian? After all, I see so-called Christians choosing evil every day of their lives."

My buddy wasn't the only one. Gandhi reportedly once said, "I like your Christ; I do not like your Christians. Your Christians are so unlike Christ."[2]

Titus 1:5–9 (The Voice):

I left you in Crete so you could sort out the chaos and the unfinished business and appoint elders *over communities* in each and every city according to my earlier orders. *Here's what you should look for in an elder:* he should be above suspicion; *if he is married he should* be the husband of one wife, raise children who believe, and be a person who can't be accused of rough and raucous living. It is necessary that any overseer *you appoint* be blameless, as he is entrusted with God's mission. *Look for someone who* isn't pompous or quick to anger, who is not a drunkard, violent, or chasing after seedy gain *or worldly fame. Find a person* who lovingly opens his home to others, who honors goodness, who is thoughtful, fair, devout, self-controlled, and who clings to the faithful Word that was taught because he must be able not only to encourage people with sound teaching, but also to challenge those who are against it.

Why was Paul so concerned about the elders in the church being blameless in the sight of God? Was he just some sort of legalist who wanted everyone to act righteously? I don't think so. I think Paul wanted elders and other people in the church to be godly, not only for God's sake but also for the sake of the world.

My dad often tells me, "When you least expect it, someone is watching you." He's right. This doesn't mean we should be paranoid or terrified. But this idea should remind us that it is a serious problem when we say we love Christ but consistently choose evil. God forgives us for our sin, but often the people with whom we want to share God's story don't forgive so quickly.

As we've heard all week, no good is not good and not good is evil. And when we go from standing still to turning back, we're actively preventing people from seeing the Cross. This is not good. Sometimes we can convince ourselves that if we choose sin, it doesn't really affect anyone else. But that's not true. If we are going to live with the name of Christ, we must count the cost, including the ways we might obstruct the Cross. Our goal should be to present a real picture of Christ to the people around us, so that people like Gandhi or my high school buddy will want to know more about Christ, not less.

by 12·28 Here's Your Challenge— Now You're on the Clock

By 12:28 tomorrow, look in the mirror. Are you turning back from Christ in any way right now? How is your turning back turning others off to Christ? Stare at the reflection you see in the mirror and take some time to honestly evaluate your life right now. Then ask God to show you what you need to do to turn around.

DAY 5: From Obstruction to Introduction

by Dave Rhodes

A few months ago, my wife and I decided to "bundle." You probably know what I'm talking about—it's the big decision to combine your cable service with your phone and Internet service. Kim and I decided to take the plunge. Now we are a fully functioning family unit with high-speed Internet, high-definition television, and high-octane long distance. (Okay, I don't know what high-octane long distance is, but it seemed like the phone company needed to keep up with TV and the Internet.)

We searched to see which company offered the best bundle. As we did, we looked not only at the service we would get and the price we would pay, but also at the incentives they were offering. One of these incentives was a free $75 Visa gift card, and that was the final straw that got us to sign on the dotted line.

We could hardly believe it when our gift card arrived. We could spend this card anywhere on anything we wanted. We put the card in a safe place and resolved not to waste this precious gem, because we wanted to use it at just the right time and in just the right place. That time and place came nine months later when Kim and I were on vacation with her family. Kim's mom offered to keep our kids while we went out to dinner. Most of the time, we would look for a restaurant in line with our budget. But not this time. It's easier to spend someone else's money, and this was the celebration night when our bundling was going to pay off.

So you can imagine the heartbreak we experienced when, right before we made our reservations, we looked at the card just to make sure everything was good to go. When we did, we saw it had expired. Now, the thing that had promised so much joy was just a cheap piece of plastic. There was no warning, no courtesy call to let us know the card was expiring. It was just a printed date that had passed by without notice.

Today's devotion is a courtesy call to let you know that your life has an expiration date. It's a call to remind you that sometimes by saving your life, you lose it, and that sometimes by spending your life, you save it. Don't let

time pass you by. If you have been living in neutral, change today. Move from being an *obstruction* to the cross to being an *introduction* to the cross. We see in today's passage how Paul did this in his journey.

1 Timothy 1:15–19 (The Voice):

Here's a statement worthy of trust: "The Liberator Jesus came into the world to save sinners," and I am the worst of them all. But it is for this reason that I was given mercy: by displaying His perfect patience in me, *the very worst of all sinners*, the Liberator Jesus could show that patience to all who would believe in Him and gain eternal life. May the King eternal, immortal, and invisible, the one and only God, now be honored and glorified forever and ever. Amen.

Timothy, my dear child, I am placing before you a charge *for the mission ahead*. It is in total agreement with the prophecies once spoken over you. *Here it is:* with God's message stirring and directing you fight the good fight, armed with faith and a good conscience. Some have tried to silence their consciences and so wrecked their lives *and ruined their* faith.

Paul wrote to his young protégé, Timothy, to give him some instructions about how to live. Paul knew that his time on earth was coming to an end, so he wrote to this young man, who had most of his life in front of him, to encourage him to spend his life on the things that mattered. This meant living as an introduction to the Cross, not an obstruction to it. Paul didn't want Timothy to wait until the perfect day to follow Jesus came, and he didn't want Timothy to shipwreck his faith. In other words, Paul wrote to encourage Timothy not to live in neutral and not to turn back to evil.

This week we've seen how no good is not good and not good is evil. Next week we'll turn the page to see what life in Christ should look like. As we close this week, we want to begin to make that move. We want to begin to chart a path that will help us make the most of our lives. We want to begin to give ourselves fully to Jesus and fall head over heels into the story of good in our world.

by 12:28 Here's Your Challenge— Now You're on the Clock

By 12:28 tomorrow, write your epitaph. Think about your life and acknowledge your expiration date. How do you want to be remembered? What things do you want to be known for? What good can you write about yourself thanks to the power of Jesus working through you? Start the journey toward goodness with Jesus today so that you can leave a legacy with your life.

SESSION

Men in Trees

Climb Down with Zacchaeus to the Root of Radical

Video Discussion

What's your mulch?

Chad describes his perfect night: a box of Cheez-Its, ESPN, and a . . . bubble bath. One night, while he was having his bubbly, he heard a low growl and "I'm gonna kill you!" emanating from the other room. He snuck in and watched his four-year-old son in a cape and mask, and nothing else, slaying imaginary foes. As children we all fought the bad guys, killed dragons, rescued girls, trekked the far reaches of the earth, and more.

> "Let go of your adult sensibilities and see a piece of God
> In a child's sense of wonder and willingness to dream
> Then a piece of God might be seen
> In a grown, short man
> Climbing a poor tree
> Dumbstruck, Zacchaeus had to be asking,
> 'How can it be
> That Thou, my God,
> would dine with me?'"

 What was your childhood fantasy? What superhero did you want to be? Why?

Along life's journey, have you lost any of your ability to dream big?

Most adults find that they have moved away from a childlike faith. Oftentimes we're encouraged to "think outside the box" or "dream big." But you never have to teach a child to think big. Instead of trying to just get through life without doing dumb things, live with childlike curiosity and simplicity. God sent His Son not so I can just sail through life, but so that I can live in an extreme level on planet earth.

 In what areas are you sailing through life, and in what areas are you living extreme?

Peter was one of the most impulsive and emotionally driven disciples. He cut off ears and made reckless promises. And one day he lunged himself out of a boat to walk on water. His faith propelled him across the lake. As a child, Chad tried to do that same thing, stepping into Uncle Jack's pond with his new white Pumas on. But when he walked into his grandma's house with soggy brown shoes on, she didn't condemn him—she smiled and shared his story.

When is the first time in your life you (or someone close to you) knew that you took God seriously?

Our culture has become so obsessed with living a balanced life. It is our ultimate goal, our biggest desire. But if you look at the people who make a difference in a major way in our world, you'll quickly notice that those people are nowhere near balanced—they are extreme, even radical. Jesus fits this description in an ultimate sense. So when did we get so afraid? Why are we trying so hard to be balanced?

Luke 19:1–10 (The Voice)

Narrator: Jesus enters Jericho and seems only to be passing through. Living in Jericho is a man named Zaccheus. He's the head tax collector and is very rich. He is also very short. He wants to see Jesus as He passes through the center of town, but he can't get a glimpse because the crowd blocks his view. So he runs ahead of the crowd and climbs up into a sycamore tree so he can see Jesus when He passes beneath him.

Jesus comes along and looks up into the tree [and there He sees Zaccheus].

Jesus: Zaccheus, hurry down from that tree because I need to stay at your house *tonight*.

Narrator: Zaccheus scrambles down and joyfully brings Jesus back to his house. Now the crowd sees this, and they're upset.

Crowd (*grumbling*): Jesus has become the houseguest of this fellow who is a notorious sinner.

Zaccheus: Lord, I am giving half of my goods to the poor, and whomever I have cheated I will pay back four times what I took.

Jesus: Today, liberation has come to this house, since even Zaccheus is living as a son of Abraham. For the Son of Man came to seek and to liberate the lost.

Do you struggle with the pressure to balance your life? When is that good and when is that bad? Or do you feel comfortable focusing your life and energy in an intentional, extreme way?

Chad talks about his treadmill phobia—of stepping one foot off the belt while you're running at Michael Johnson speed. But the truth about treadmills is that they're stationary—we run on them but never go anywhere. But Jesus was never stationary; the cross was not meant to be stationary. God wants us to live the life He intended us to live. He has given us freedom and power and authority, and we have the opportunity to experience it. The truth is, we're scared to death to believe it, because if we do, then we're held accountable.

 Why are we held more accountable when we embrace the freedom, power, and authority God has for us?

Followers of Christ—not mere "believers"—buy their friends lunch when they don't have money to spare. They pray for ten minutes when they only have thirty seconds to give. If we don't understand the power invested in us, we won't be able to understand the extreme freedom God gives us. The landscaper who worked on Chad's yard for free knew what he had available to give—mulch. That was his gift. He gave it in an extreme way.

 What is your mulch? And if you don't know, who in your life can help you figure that out?

 What would you have to do to catch God off guard with your life?

Daily Readings

DAY 1: Catching Jesus Off Guard

by Chad Norris

I communicate for a living. Since God called me to preach almost twenty years ago, I've had the opportunity to speak many times in many places. In fact, I travel and speak so much that sometimes I don't know where I even am, because the events seem to run together.

This summer, I traveled to several camps to preach, as I normally do. I decided to take my four-year-old, Sam, to some of these camps so that we could have some father-son time. At one of these camps, I was getting ready to speak to about one thousand students. During the worship time before my talk, there was a soft song, and I walked out on stage to worship with the band. It was a really holy moment, and none of us wanted to move. But then something shocking happened.

I looked out at the center aisle and saw my son Sam there. He had made his way from the back of the room, where he was sitting with some camp staffers, and he was now worshiping in the middle of all these students. This may not sound like a big deal to you, but it really surprised me. Sam is pretty shy and reserved by nature, and so it floored me to see him do this. He caught me off guard, and it is one of the sweetest moments I've had as a father.

Matthew 14:25–29 (The Voice):

Narrator: Deep in the night, *when He had concluded His prayers,* Jesus walked out on the water to His disciples *in their boat.* The disciples saw a figure moving toward them and were terrified.
Disciple: It's a ghost!
Another Disciple: A ghost? *What will we do?*
Jesus: Be still. It is I. You have nothing to fear.
Peter: Lord, if it is really You, then command me to meet You on the water.
Jesus: *Indeed,* come.

Do you think it's possible to catch Jesus off guard? I think that might have happened in this passage. Jesus was walking on water toward his disciples, and most of them were terrified. But Peter actually stepped out of the boat onto the water and began walking toward Jesus.

Don't miss this! Peter believed in Jesus so much that he was willing to try to walk on water to get to Him. Can you imagine what Jesus' inner dialogue was like? I would guess it was something like, *I can't believe Peter actually tried this. I'm impressed!*

I can't say for sure whether Jesus was caught off guard by Peter's faith. Maybe He was, and maybe He wasn't. But, I would bet that the other disciples were caught off guard. And I can promise you that we can live out our faith in ways that catch others off guard. This week we'll talk about how we can soar to places of extravagance and ask, "What's your mulch?" In other words, what gifts has God given you, and how can you use those gifts in extravagant ways to change our world? What goodness can you plot in the world to bring redemption and hope to those around you?

by 12:28 Here's Your Challenge— Now You're on the Clock

By 12:28 tomorrow, dream extravagantly. Make a list below of three extravagant things you want to do in the next three months. Then begin dreaming about how you will catch someone off guard by doing these things in the coming days and weeks.

1. _____
2. _____
3. _____

DAY 2: Extravagant Collection

by Dave Rhodes

Almost everyone I know wanted to be a superhero when they grew up. Some of us wanted to fly like Superman and save the day. Others of us wanted to swing between buildings like Spider-Man and save the girl. Still others of us *were* the girl and wanted to be Wonder Woman, deflecting our foes' bullets with our bracelets as we saved the world.

I think that all of us remember what it was like to want to be a superhero. You remember tying a towel around your neck and diving off your top bunk, really expecting to fly like Superman. You remember throwing yourself up against the wall, really expecting to stick like Spider-Man. You remember riding around in your invisible jet (which really was invisible, because it was imaginary) like Wonder Woman, really expecting others to be awestruck by how you were traveling like that. We all did these things, and I think it's because there's something inside of us that wants to find our special power and make a difference in the world.

But as we remember these superheroes, do you remember the place where these Super Friends came together? It was the place where Batman and Robin met with Aquaman and the Wonder Twins. It's the place where Superman and Wonder Woman hung out together. Of course, we're talking about the Hall of Justice. In this place, all sorts of different superheroes with all kinds of special powers came together to plot goodness in the world. Some had innate powers that enabled them to do amazing things. Others, like Green Lantern or the Wonder Twins, only had a special ring or could turn into something stupid like a bucket of water. But all of them worked together as a special collection to do together what they couldn't do on their own.

Do you think the Super Friends were onto something with their Hall of Justice? Is it possible in some weird way that these heroes can give us a picture of what the community of God is supposed to be about? Is it possible that we have special powers of some kind? Is it possible that we are all part of this extravagant collection that God wants to use to plot goodness in the world? And is it possible that God is waiting for us to play our role in this extravagant collection?

---

1 Corinthians 12:4–27 (The Voice):

Now there are many kinds of grace-gifts out there, but they are all from the same Spirit. There are many different service-gifts, but *they're all directed by* the same Lord. There are many amazing working-gifts in the church, but it is the same God who energizes them all in all *who have the gifts.*

Each believer has received a gift that manifests the Spirit's *power and presence.* That gift is given for the good of the whole community. The Spirit gives one person a word of wisdom, but to the next person the same Spirit gives a word of knowledge. Another will receive *the gift of* faith by the same Spirit, and still another gifts of healing—all from the one Spirit. One person is enabled *by the Spirit* to perform miracles, another to prophesy, while another is enabled to distinguish *those prophetic* spirits. The next one speaks in various kinds of tongues, while another is able to interpret those tongues. One Spirit works all these things in each of them individually as He sees fit.

Just as a body is one whole made up of many different parts, and all the different parts comprise the one body, so it is with our Liberating King. We were all ceremonially washed together into one body by one Spirit. *No matter our heritage*—Jew or outsider—*no matter our status*—oppressed or free—we were all given the one Spirit to drink. *Here's why:* The body is not made of one large part but of many *different parts.* Would it seem right for the foot to cry, "I am not a hand, so I couldn't be part of this body"? Even if it did, it wouldn't be any less joined to the body. And what about an ear? If an ear started to whine, "I am not an eye; I shouldn't be attached to this body," in all its pouting it is still part of the body. Imagine the entire body as an eye. How would a giant eye have the sense to hear? And if the entire body were an ear, how would it have the sense to smell? *This is where God comes in.* God has meticulously put this body together; He placed each part in the exact place to perform the exact function He wanted. If all members were a single part, where would the body be? So now, many members *function* within the one body. The eye cannot wail at the hand, "I have no need for you," nor could the head bellow at the feet, "I won't go one more step with you." It's actually the opposite. The members who seem to have the weaker functions are necessary to keep the body moving; the body parts that seem less important we treat as some of the most valuable, and those unfit, untamed, unpresentable members we treat with an even greater modesty. That's something the more presentable members don't need. But God designed the body in such a way that greater significance is given to the *seemingly* insignificant part. That way there should be no division in the body; instead, all the parts share a mutual dependence and mutual care for each other. If one part is suffering, then all the members suffer alongside it. If one member is honored, then all the members celebrate alongside it. You are the body of our Liberating King; each and every one of you is a *lifetime* member.

So what's your mulch? What are your gifts? The truth today is that the kingdom of God needs you to play your role. God's extravagant collection isn't complete unless you do your part. If you're a toe, be the best toe you can be. If you're an arm, be the best arm you can be. And as you're out there being the best you can be, you're also partnering with God to write the story of true goodness—a story that, in the end, saves the day, the girl, and the world.

by 12:28 Here's Your Challenge— Now You're on the Clock

By 12:28 tomorrow, plot goodness. Ask one person to tell you what he or she thinks your unique gifts and attributes are, and then make a plan about how you can use at least one of these gifts or attributes to be a part of the story of goodness. Also, tell one other person something unique that you see in him or her, and challenge that person to use his or her gift or attribute to plot goodness as well.

DAY 3: Extravagant Connection

by Chris Brooks

I had an expensive camera in my hand, and that was probably my first mistake.

I was filming two guys from a worship band named Spur58, and that was probably my second mistake.

Normally, I wouldn't be caught dead filming yet another edgy, trendy-looking worship band that is contributing to the false hero-worship that has replaced character with celebrity, but these two guys from Spur58 were different. The setting was different, too.

We were in Lima, Peru, hiking up to the home of the children whom Aaron Ivey and Steven Bush (of Spur 58) sponsor through Compassion International. These children are sisters who live on the side of a sandy mountain in one of the poorest urban areas in the world. This ghetto of plastic shacks and tin roofs made the lighting less than ideal, and there was no sanitation, no stairs, and no running water. I was quickly overwhelmed by the hopelessness of it all.

I hid behind the camera, content to be an observer, as we arrived at a ten-by-twenty-foot shack that housed five family members. The pixilated scene I saw through the camera's eyepiece seemed inadequate to capture the reality that was in front of me. But then something amazing and unexpected and radical happened. As Aaron and Steven began to give their children simple gifts like lip gloss, jump ropes, and a feathery boa, the girls lit up like it was Christmas morning. The girls danced and sang and laughed like all kids their age should—like kids in their living conditions usually don't. Their mom tearfully explained in Spanish that her only hope in life was from the kindness of these strangers and the Compassion program that gave her children the opportunity to make a better life for themselves.

The connection between Aaron and Steve and this Peruvian family was radically different from anything I had ever witnessed. It changed me in a way I still haven't gotten over.

Luke 19:1–10 (The Voice):

Narrator: Jesus enters Jericho and seems only to be passing through. Living in Jericho is a man named Zaccheus. He's the head tax collector and is very rich. He is also very short. He wants to see Jesus as He passes through the center of town, but he can't get a glimpse because the crowd blocks his view. So he runs ahead of the crowd and climbs up into a sycamore tree so he can see Jesus when He passes beneath him.

Jesus comes along and looks up into the tree [and there He sees Zaccheus].

Jesus: Zaccheus, hurry down from that tree because I need to stay at your house *tonight*.

Narrator: Zaccheus scrambles down and joyfully brings Jesus back to his house. Now the crowd sees this, and they're upset.

Crowd (*grumbling*): Jesus has become the houseguest of this fellow who is a notorious sinner.

Zaccheus: Lord, I am giving half of my goods to the poor, and whomever I have cheated I will pay back four times what I took.

Jesus: Today, liberation has come to this house, since even Zaccheus is living as a son of Abraham. For the Son of Man came to seek and to liberate the lost.

What we sometimes miss in this story of Zacchaeus is the radical and extravagant connection that formed between two very unlikely people. This tax collector, who was basically like a notorious rich mobster to the Jewish people, connected with an edgy rabbi who dared not only to talk with him but to dine with him as well. For Jewish people, a meal was considered an invitation to begin a friendship and an opportunity for deep connection. And we see in this story that Zacchaeus was so overwhelmed during this meal by Jesus' extravagant gesture of grace and forgiveness that he re-sponded by extravagantly giving away his gifts. Zacchaeus's "mulch" was money, and he gave it away freely.

My motivation for extravagance is much like Zacchaeus's motivation. I have entered the story of good and extravagant living because I still can't get over the wonderful truth that Jesus wants to connect with me. He not only loves me—he likes me. So I will dig deep into my pockets, into my life, into my gifts, and into my mulch to shower the world with the wealth I have hoarded for far too long.

As we got up to leave the home of our hosts in Peru, the mother seemed to be at a loss to express her gratitude. Of course, despite the language barrier, her face communicated everything we needed to know. But that was not enough for her. Her daughters had been infected by compassion and hope for the future. So she reached over and handed Aaron a simple handmade basket and said, *"Muchas gracias."* Humbled and taken aback but aware that it would be rude to refuse, Aaron reluctantly accepted the small gift.

As we made our way back down the dusty incline, I was trying to process basic things, like the meaning of life and how I could partner with Compassion International to eradicate global poverty. Then I overheard the translator explain to Aaron that the basket he held in his hands had been made by the mother. She sold these baskets at the market, and it was her family's sole source of income. She had just given Aaron one month of her wages in thanks for the extravagant connection he had made with her family. Amazing!

12:2 Here's Your Challenge— Now You're on the Clock

By 12:28 tomorrow, connect the dots. Think about who has made an extravagant connection with you in the past, either through love, time, or a gift, and thank God for that person. Then ask God to show you someone with whom He wants you to extravagantly connect. Pray about how and when you can do this.

DAY 4: Extravagant Reflection

by Dave Rhodes

They say that imitation is the greatest form of flattery. In other words, it's natural for us to follow the lead of someone we respect or want to be like. I found this to be true the other day when I was mowing my yard. I'm not a big outdoorsman, but I do have a tractor—a lawn tractor, that is. After push-mowing our half-acre lot for two years, I finally realized that the whole neighborhood was laughing at me, so I broke down and made the big purchase. Now, mowing the yard is fun for me, as I ride around drinking a glass of lemonade and feeling like a real man sitting on a piece of heavy machinery. Pretty much every Saturday in the spring and summer, I get on my tractor and do the "guy duty" of mowing our yard.

About three years ago, my daughter Emma also got a tractor. My brother-in-law's mother works for John Deere, and she gave Emma a miniature John Deere riding tractor for her birthday so that Emma could mow the yard with her dad. For the past few years, Emma and I have mowed the yard together. At first, things were pretty predictable. I mowed the yard, and Emma just drove her tractor around. She didn't follow any pattern, and she had trouble steering. She ran over plants and shrubs and endangered everything around her.

But a few weeks ago, I noticed Emma doing something I had never seen her do before. I looked behind me as I mowed and saw Emma following my tracks. She took the same turns that I did. She followed my pattern. She watched me intently to see what my next move would be, and then she imitated it. I was stunned at what I was watching. I hadn't told Emma to do this. I didn't coax or trick her into following me. She just wanted to be like her dad, so she followed my tracks. All morning, my mini-me rode about twenty yards behind me, imitating my every move and having the time of her life doing it.

So here's the question today: Who are you imitating? Whose path are you following? And if people were to follow or imitate you, where would they be headed?

Ephesians 5:1–2 (The Voice):

So imitate God. *Follow Him* like adored children, and live in love as Christ loved you—so much that He gave Himself as a fragrant sacrifice, pleasing God.

Paul wrote this letter to the Ephesian church. This church was doing some pretty amazing things. Unlike most of Paul's letters, Ephesians doesn't address any particular error or heresy. Instead, Paul wrote to encourage these people in their walk with Christ. And in these two verses, Paul got to what I think is the linchpin of the whole letter. As he told the Christians at Ephesus how to live, he told them to imitate Christ.

That's what this week is all about—following in Christ's tracks. It's about being extravagant reflections of who He is. It's about being His mini-me, so to speak. This is a simple thought, but it's incredibly challenging.

 ## Here's Your Challenge— Now You're on the Clock

By 12:28 tomorrow, follow Jesus' tracks. Make a list below of some of the things Jesus did throughout the New Testament. Pick one thing you think you can do, and then do it. Afterward, journal about your experience. Keep this list, and if you have the courage, find a few more things that God can help you imitate. As you do this, remember that you are extravagantly reflecting Christ to the world.

DAY 5: Your Extravagance

by Chad Norris

"You're a good listener."

I'll never forget the moment my brother said this to me. It happened about ten years ago, and I still haven't forgotten it. It was as if God had said it to me.

As Christians, we are challenged to give our lives away consistently. We know this often means money; it did for Zacchaeus. But being extravagant is about much more than money. All week, we've been asking one question: What's your mulch? In other words, what's the way that you can extravagantly join the story of goodness God is writing in the world?

Since the day my brother told me I was a good listener, I've tried to give my listening away. That may sound ridiculous, but it's a reality. Hopefully this will give you a picture of how broad the idea of being extravagant really is. God is calling us to be extravagant with all of the gifts and abilities and character traits He has blessed us with, and it's time for us to unleash this extravagance right now.

John 13:1–5 (The Voice):

Before the Passover festival began, Jesus was keenly aware that His hour had come to depart from this world and to return to the Father. From beginning to end, Jesus' days were marked by His love for His people. Before Jesus and His disciples gathered for dinner, the adversary filled Judas Iscariot's heart with plans of deceit and betrayal. Jesus, knowing that He had come from God and was going away to God, stood up from dinner and removed His outer garments. He then wrapped Himself in a towel, poured water in a basin, and began to wash the feet of the disciples, drying them with His towel.

What do you think of when you think about Christ? Do you picture Him walking on water? Healing the sick? Raising the dead? Jesus was supernatural, and He did many amazing, extravagant things. But the image of Him that's burned in my mind is Him as a foot washer. The King of the universe washed dirty feet. It boggles my mind.

When it comes to living extravagantly, our ultimate example is Jesus. He lived and gave and loved extravagantly, and He challenges us to do so as well. Most of us don't have millions of dollars like Zacchaeus, but we can catch Jesus off guard by living extravagantly as well. Maybe you're a great encourager—then encourage. Maybe you can wash a car better than anyone—then do it. If you're a great listener like me, let it rip. We can all bless others with what we have, and we can do it extravagantly. We all have mulch, so no matter what form it takes, use it to be extravagant in bringing the good story of God to the world around you.

by 12:28 Here's Your Challenge— Now You're on the Clock

By 12:28 tomorrow, get extravagant. This week you have dreamed extravagantly, plotted goodness, connected the dots, and followed Jesus' tracks, so you already know what you need to do. Now take the challenge and do something extravagant to spread whatever your mulch is into the world.

SESSION

The Living Tree

Hear from Heaven . . . Join the Movement

Video Discussion

Pass the piece.

All of us come from different traditions in the way we worship. Some of us prefer structure and order, and others prefer creativity and spontaneity. Chris's story about doing the sign of the cross is funny and ridiculous, but we've all encountered new situations that were intimidating or, at the least, unfamiliar to us before.

Describe a time when you were embarrassed or confused in a church setting.

"So the dominos continue to fall
The dominos continue to drop
    Forward into the story of
        good and evil
Two stories clickety-clacketing
    forward
In a furious race for your time
Begging you not to pantomime
    Religious rules and
        regulations
    Or mirrored regurgitations
But giving everything
    you've got
It may not be much
It may not be mulch
But a decision must be made
        today and every day

Because no good—
        That's not good
And not good is evil
That is to say, neutrality
That's no longer an option
And much to our dismay
Jesus—He's still on His way."

Revelation 22:1–7 (The Voice):

John: My heavenly guide brought me to the river of *pure* living waters, *shimmering as* brilliant as crystal. It flowed out from the throne of God and of the Lamb flowing down the middle and dividing the street of the holy city. On each bank of the river stood the tree of life, *firmly planted*, bearing 12 kinds of fruit and producing its sweet crop every month *throughout the year*. And the *soothing* leaves that grew on the tree *of life* provided precious healing for the nations.

Narrator: No one or nothing will labor under any curse any longer. And the throne of God and of the Lamb will sit *prominently* in the city. God's servants will *continually* serve *and worship* Him. They will be able to look upon His face, and His name will be written on their foreheads. And darkness will never again fall *on this city*. They will not require the light of a lamp or of the sun because the Lord God will be their illumination. *By His light*, they will reign throughout the ages.

Guide (*speaking to me*)**:** These words are faithful and true, for the Lord, the God who inspired the prophets, has sent His heavenly messenger to show to His servants what must soon take place.

The One: Look now, I am coming soon! The one who remains true to the prophetic words contained in this book will truly be blessed.

Many of us are given an image of heaven that is all cherubs and clouds and streets of gold and percussion instruments. From our earliest childhood we think we'll be singing songs and "praising God" all day long. As Chris said in the video, "The idea of heaven scared me more than the thought of hell. Perpetual Sundays with perpetual services from which there would be no escape." But this is not the glimpse of heaven that God gives us when he pulls back the curtain in Revelation 22.

Jesus had to deal with a lot of preconceived notions about heaven with the religious establishment of His day. But His idea was better than any they had imagined. He taught them to risk greatly. Love deeply. Let go to gain your life. God has not given up on His creation or His created. There is resurrection power coming to this earth.

 In what ways have you given up on this earth?

We were imprinted with a crystal clear image of God, but it was marred, smudged, blurred at the Fall. But when we start to understand that this world is wired for high-def but is still getting its reception on rabbit ears, that's when we realize our role in making this a better world. *Pimp My Ride* shows us a picture of restoration in creativity—not in making something new, but in bringing beauty out of something that was already there.

 In what ways do you long to bring beauty out in this world?

Getting a glimpse of before and after scenes gives us the courage to whisper, "What if?" Heaven is not static but dynamic. It's a tale of unending adventure, splendor, glory, and increased intimacy. What if our pets are there? What if Jesus compared heaven to eating, drinking, and celebrating because that's what we'll be doing when we're there? Or maybe because they're the most intense human desires we'll experience on earth, and we'll live in those moments there as well.

What is your "what if" dream about heaven?

What if right now, by the way we're living our lives, we're literally laying the foundations of an eternal city? What if we are not going to heaven, but heaven is coming to earth? A piece of it was given to us, and we have access to it. This is a great responsibility—not something to take lightly.

 What are you doing with the piece of God that He has given you?

The dominos have fallen, but they have been reversed. And now we've been given a piece of God, and it's our right, our privilege, and our divine responsibility to do something with it. We must be active participants in passing the piece and passing the domino. Today you have been given a domino, to pass the piece of God to someone who is actively participating in the Story of Goodness in our world. This story can be tracked at passthedomino.com as we invite you to fall forward into the Story of Goodness.

 How will you pass a piece of God on to someone else *today*—**before you go to bed tonight?**

DAY 1: Pass the Domino

by Chris Brooks

This week we're going to talk about passing the domino, or to use a play on words, passing the piece. This pun refers to the liturgical tradition of passing the peace of God as part of worship, and it also points to the piece of God and his kingdom that the Holy Spirit has placed in our hearts. The domino game piece represents the piece of God's kingdom with which we have been entrusted, and it reminds us of our commission to pass it on. You can read more about the *Domino Effect* and the ways people are passing the dominos at www.passthedomino.com, and you can share your story there as well. It may seem weird at first to pass a domino piece to someone, but it's actually quite natural to pass along something you have experienced. You might even say it is human nature.

For instance, if you are out with some friends, eating a nice meal, and you take a bite of something extraordinary, what's usually your first reaction? "Oh my gosh—you've got to taste this!" You pass a piece of whatever you taste so that someone else can share this great experience with you. This can also work in reverse, especially for guys. If a guy tastes or smells something awful, he wants all his guy friends to share in the foulness. Passing a piece of what we experience is natural.

That's why it's so tragic that so many of us were passed a piece of God that didn't exactly taste right. This happened to me, especially when it comes to God's plans for his kingdom and for heaven. Someone passed me the interpretation that heaven was bland and boring, full of chubby cherubs, clouds, harps, and a lot of gaudy gold and bleached-out whites. I thought everyone in heaven would float around and pretend we enjoyed singing all day, every day for the rest of eternity. But the glimpses and pieces of heaven we see in Scripture stand in stark contrast to the sanitized version I was passed.

Revelation 21:1–5 (The Voice):

John: I looked again *and could hardly believe my eyes.* Everything above me was new. Everything below me was new. Everything around me was new because the heaven and earth that had been had passed away, and the sea was gone, completely. And I saw the holy city, the new Jerusalem, descending out of heaven from God, prepared like a bride *on her wedding day*, adorned for her Husband *and for His eyes only*. And I heard a great voice, coming from the throne announcing:

"See, the home of God is with *His* people.
He will live among them;
　　they will be His people,
　　and God Himself will be with them.
The prophecies are fulfilled:
　　He will wipe away every tear from their eyes.
Death will be no more;
　　mourning no more, crying no more, pain no more,
　　for the first things have gone away."

And the one who sat on the throne announced *to His creation*, "See, I am making all things new." *Turning to me* He said, "Write *what you hear and see*, for these words are faithful and true."

Heaven is coming to earth! God's resurrection power is so much greater than we give Him credit for. The insurrection of the resurrection has begun with the risen Jesus, the firstfruits of the resurrection. Our problem comes when we think that heaven isn't going to be a real place on this real, resurrected earth occupied by our real, resurrected bodies, and it's even worse to think we have no access to this resurrection power until the final resurrection takes place.

The reality is that the same power that raised Jesus from the grave lives in us. This isn't just a statement designed to make you feel better about your life—it's a divine call of your responsibility to pass the piece and the resurrection power of God to those around you. "Your will be done on earth as it is in heaven," is the way Jesus put it, and that's what happens when we, the church, pass the piece.

We have the opportunity and the commission to bring heaven to earth as we start enacting God's rule and reign by the way we love Him and love one another. Heaven and hell are realities. Good and evil are realities. And the awful reality is that some people are experiencing pieces of hell and evil right now because we have failed to fulfill our job as peace-passers. So pass the piece and let someone savor the reality of heaven today.

by 12:28 Here's Your Challenge— Now You're on the Clock

By 12:28 tomorrow, pass the piece. Begin by praying about whom you will pass your domino to and why you should pass it to that person. Ask God to bring someone who has been a tangible expression of His love and peace to your mind. Then tell that person specifically, either out loud or in a letter, how he or she brought heaven to earth for you or someone else. Stress the importance of that person passing the piece along to someone who does the same thing for him or her. Let this person know that, because he or she passed the piece, you are now caught up in the domino effect of good overcoming evil.

DAY 2: No Matter What

by Chad Norris

I love drama. I love watching movies that build to climactic scenes where Rudy, Rocky, Braveheart, and the Gladiator win the day. I love watching movies like *The Notebook* where the guy and the girl fall in love. I think this is one of the reasons I love the Bible so much. The Bible is full of stories, and these stories are full of drama. There are heroes and villains, laughter and tears, highs and lows. You name it, and it's in there. Today, we're going to look at one of those dramatic stories.

Esther 4:1–17 (The Voice):

Narrator: *Mordecai mourned* when he found out what had happened. He ripped his clothes to shreds. He put on sackcloth and wiped ash onto his body. Then he went through the city, weeping loudly in anguish. When he came to the king's gate, *not far from the royal harem,* he stopped since those wearing sackcloth weren't allowed to enter it *and disrupt the merriment of the court.*

In the meantime, as word of the new decree began to spread throughout all of the king's provinces, terrible distress grew among the Jews. They stopped eating. They wept. They screamed out in misery. *Like Mordecai,* many of them laid in *heaps of* sackcloth and ashes.

Esther's maids and eunuchs *witnessed Mordecai mourning outside of the king's gate.* They went and reported to the queen all that they saw.

Esther: *Why does he mourn?* This troubles me. My heart breaks. Take these clothes to Mordecai so he can put them on instead of wearing sackcloth.

Narrator: *But when the servants returned to the gate,* Mordecai refused to wear the clothes *Queen Esther had sent.* Meanwhile, Esther sent for Hathach who was one of the king's eunuchs assigned to serve her.

Esther: Hathach, go to Mordecai at once. Find out why he is mourning, *and report back to me all that he says.*

Narrator: Hathach went to Mordecai in the open square of the city in front of the king's gate. Mordecai told the queen's servant everything that had happened to him.

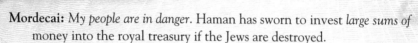

Mordecai: *My people are in danger.* Haman has sworn to invest *large sums of money* into the royal treasury if the Jews are destroyed.

(handing Hathach a scroll): Here, this is a copy of the law *proving all that I am telling you.* It's basically an order for genocide. It's being posted *as we speak* all over the city of Susa. Show it to Esther. Tell her everything I have told you. Convince her to go before her king and plead *for mercy, not only for her life, but also* for the lives of her people.

Narrator: Hathach returned to Esther and told her everything that Mordecai said.

Esther: *Return to the city's gate, Hathach, and* deliver this message to Mordecai: *"How am I supposed to see the king?* It's known *throughout the kingdom,* from the greatest of the king's officials to the common folk who live in the royal provinces, that any person who approaches the king in the inner chamber without being invited is sentenced to death. That's the law! There's only one exception, and that's if the king were to hold out the gold scepter to that person and spare his or her life. It's been 30 days since the king has summoned me!"

Narrator: Hathach took Esther's response to Mordecai.

Mordecai: Tell Esther, "Don't be fooled. Just because you are living inside the king's palace doesn't mean that you out of all of the Jews will escape *the carnage. You must go before your king.* If you stay quiet during this time, hope and liberation for our people will come from somewhere, but *in the meantime,* you, *my child,* and all of your father's flesh and blood will be put to death. And who knows? Perhaps you have been made queen for such a time as this."

Narrator: *Once again, Hathach returned to Queen Esther.*

Esther: Go and tell Mordecai, *"I understand. In preparation for my audience with the king,* do this: gather together all the Jews in Susa, and fast *and pray* for me. For three days and nights, cleanse your bodies of all food and drink. My maids and I will join you in this time of cleansing. And after the three days, I will break the law and go before my king *to plead my people's case.* And if I die, then I die!

Narrator: Mordecai left *the entrance of the king's gate* and put all of Esther's instructions into action.

Talk about drama! A Jewish girl grew up to become a beautiful woman, and her beauty made her the queen of a foreign land. God had put her in a position from which she could be the savior of His people. A jealous, petty official put together a plan to wipe out the Jews, but little did he know while he composed his evil tale that God was already writing a story of good and redemption and hope.

This story was coming to its dramatic apex. Esther had to choose whether she would risk her life to push the dominos toward good or give up and let the evil story continue. She decided that no matter what, she would try to write a story for good. If she died, she died, but she was going to act.

Have you ever considered the idea that you are in a drama? God might have already put you in position to pass a piece of God just like Esther did. Your story might look different from Esther's, but it is still full of good and evil, and you're right in the middle of it. You are on earth right now for a reason. You have an opportunity to walk with God and flip dominos just like Esther did. It won't be safe. It won't be easy. It wasn't for Esther! She could have died, but God saved her. And she saved an entire race of people.

Esther put herself on the line and went for it. You and I face the same opportunity all the time. I hope I can live with the same courage that Esther had and pass the domino as she did. Who knows—maybe God has us all here for such a time as this.

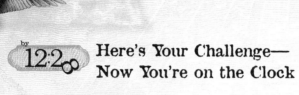

by
12:28 Here's Your Challenge—
Now You're on the Clock

By 12:28 tomorrow, ask for courage. Look honestly at the situation you're in and ask God to give you the courage you need to pass the domino. Then take the courage God gives you and act out of it.

DAY 3: Above and Beyond

by Chris Brooks

Have you ever made a bold prediction only to be proven wrong? Have you ever been limited by your circumstances and blinded by your lack of imagination and had that cause you to make a bold and foolish statement? Well, if you have, take heart—at least it wasn't as bad as these predictions:

- "Radio has no future . . . X-rays are clearly a hoax . . . The aeroplane is scientifically impossible." —Royal Society president William Thomson, Lord Kelvin, in 1897–1899
- "We don't like their sound. Groups of guitars are on the way out." —A Decca Records executive, as he turned down signing the Beatles in 1962
- "It will be years—not in my time—before a woman will become Prime Minister." —Future British Prime Minister Margaret Thatcher in 1974
- "You ought to go back to driving a truck." —A concert manager who fired Elvis Presley in 1954
- "There is not the slightest indication that nuclear energy will ever be obtainable. It would mean that the atom would have to be shattered at will." —Albert Einstein in 1932
- "The concept is interesting and well-formed, but in order to earn better than a C, the idea must be feasible." —A Yale University management professor who failed Fred Smith on a paper proposing an overnight delivery service. Smith used the idea to start FedEx
- "Market research reports say America likes crispy cookies, not soft and chewy cookies like you make." —A company's response to Debbi Fields, who later started Mrs. Fields Cookies
- "Hey, we don't need you. You haven't got through college yet." —Hewlett-Packard executives to Steve Jobs, who was pitching a personal computer idea that was later used to start Apple
- "Everything that can be invented has been invented." —Charles H. Duell, commissioner of the US Office of Patents in 1899

Never underestimate what people can do. In fact, sometimes all it takes for a great thing to happen is for someone to say that it can't happen. And sometimes all it takes for a great thing to happen is for people to give what they've got.

Exodus 36:2–7 (The Voice):

Narrator: Moses gathered Bezalel, Oholiab, every talented person whom the Eternal One had blessed with skills *and wisdom*, and all the people who were inspired to help out with the construction work. *It was not forced labor like they had experienced under the oppression of Pharaoh; this work and creativity was to come only from the willingness of their hearts.* Moses gave the craftsmen all the materials the Israelites donated to build the sacred space. *But the donations didn't stop there.* The people continued giving new offerings each morning. *In fact, the donations were so heavy that it began to impede the workers' progress.* Eventually, all the craftsmen working on the sanctuary left their particular jobs and reported *the situation* to Moses.

Workers: The people are bringing so many offerings—too many, in fact. There is more than enough material to complete the sanctuary the Eternal One has instructed us to build. *The people have been so generous, but the overflow of materials is becoming a problem. Please do something.*

Narrator: So Moses gave a new instruction, and it spread quickly throughout the entire camp.

Moses: We do not need any more materials for the construction of the sanctuary. *We have more than enough.*

Narrator: And so everyone was kept from donating more materials because the materials already in their possession were more than enough to build the sanctuary.

I'm sure that many people had written off the Hebrew people as a doomed bunch of former slaves who had no land and only one God. It would have been easy to think it would never work. But they were wrong.

Sure, these traveling Israelites were hugely inconsistent and easily lured away from God, but they proved everyone who discounted them woefully wrong. The generosity these former slaves showed in this passage was so great that Moses had to stop them because they were giving too much. When was the last time you heard your preacher tell you to stop giving because it was too much?

Much like the ancient world looked down on the Hebrew people, it seems today that the secular world has a low opinion of the church and its chance for success. For the most part, people have written off Christians as a judgmental, self-centered group of relics with no relevance for postmodern times. The church, they would say, has devolved into a safe haven for the moral elite, and it's incompetent to solve any major problems like poverty, the AIDS epidemic, or environmental responsibility.

But I just love it when I think someone is writing me off. Church historian Thomas Nelson once said that during the first century, many educated people would have thought that this new religion called Christianity or The Way would never last because it was a religion of slaves and women. It wouldn't last because its main adherents were the last, the least, and the lost. But the first-century church proved the critics wrong, and I think the time has come for the twenty-first-century church to prove the critics wrong.

What if the church decided to rise up and take its rightful place as the bride of Christ? What if we began to create a society—or kingdom, if you will—where generosity, sacrifice, and benevolence are the norm? What if the church became a place where we start to partner with others to start a domino effect of change and redemption fueled by resurrection power? What if the church became a place that not only believed the local church is the hope of the world . . . but actually lived like it? What if the church became a place where passing the piece happened every day? What if this started with your church?

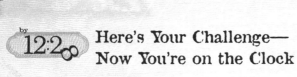

Here's Your Challenge—
Now You're on the Clock

By 12:28 tomorrow, prove them wrong. Get together with your small group or your circle of friends and start to give until someone has to tell you to stop. As the Lord stirs your hearts, begin to brainstorm and dream about how you can overwhelm someone with your giving. Start by making a list of what critics might say is wrong with your church, your community, or your world. Then pick a project, adopt a cause, or minister to a family or a person in need with your skills, talents, abilities, and resources. Keep passing the piece until someone tells you to stop because it's just too much.

DAY 4: It's Just Lunch

by Dave Rhodes

If you've been around Christianity for very long at all, I'm sure you've heard this story we're looking at today. In fact, it's the only miracle story besides the Resurrection that's retold in all four Gospels. This may tell us that this story is central to our understanding of Jesus and the way He works in our lives and our world.

John 6:5–12 (The Voice):

Narrator: But when Jesus looked up, He could see an immense crowd coming toward Him. Jesus approached Philip.

Jesus *(to Philip)*: Where is a place to buy bread so these people may eat?

Narrator: Jesus knew what He was planning to do, but He asked Philip nonetheless. He had something to teach, and it started with a test.

Philip: I could work for more than half of a year and still not have the money to buy enough bread to give each person a very small piece.

Narrator: Andrew, the disciple who was Simon Peter's brother, spoke up.

Andrew: I met a young boy in the crowd carrying five barley loaves and two fish, but that is practically useless in feeding a crowd this large.

Jesus: Tell the people to sit down.

Narrator: They all sat together on a large grassy area. *Those counting the people reported* approximately 5,000 men—*not counting the women and children*—sitting in the crowd. Jesus picked up the bread, gave thanks to God, and passed it to everyone. He repeated this ritual with the fish. *Men, women, and children* all ate to their heart's content. When the people had all they could eat, He told the disciples *to gather the leftovers*.

Jesus and the disciples were in a pretty interesting situation. From the other Gospels, we know that the disciples had just returned from one of their first mission trips. They had been following in Jesus' footsteps and doing the kinds of things that Jesus had been doing. Things had gone pretty well, and now they were looking for some rest and relaxation so they could celebrate the work Jesus was doing.

But then the people started coming again. They couldn't get enough of this new God movement. It's no surprise that this mass of people created some major crowd-control issues. It was getting dark, and no one had eaten. Out of the large crowd, the only food the disciples could find was one boy's lunch. He had just five barley loaves and two fish. The disciples told Jesus that this was practically useless in feeding a crowd that large, but Jesus knew that this bit of food was exactly what He needed to feed the crowd. Just a few verses later, we see that five thousand men plus more women and children ate from this one kid's lunch.

In this story, we see the calling for our lives. We may not have much, but what we have can be a lot in Jesus' hands. *It's just lunch*, but with our five loaves and two fish, we can pass the piece and be part of the story of goodness in the world. And if you don't believe that just lunch can make a difference, listen to these stories:

It's just shoes, but don't tell that to Blake Mycoskie. Blake was on vacation in Argentina when he got the idea to start a shoe company. But his shoe company is unlike any other. Inspired by Argentinean-style shoes, but even more by how many Argentineans don't have shoes, Blake started a company with a simple goal—for every pair of shoes he sold, he would give another pair away. Even more, Blake thought that everyone deserved to be measured for the correct size shoes and to have their new shoes placed on their feet. So he and his group individually place shoes on the feet of people who have no shoes. The company started in 2006, and in its first year it gave away ten thousand pairs of shoes, even before it became profitable. Now his official title is Chief Shoe Giver. So you may say it's just shoes, but I say that for those who have not had shoes, it's a whole new way of walking.[1]

It's just pajamas, but don't tell that to Genevieve Piturro. I saw her story on *Oprah*. (I know that's not very masculine, but my wife was watching, and I got caught up in it.) Genevieve was a single woman climbing her way up the corporate ladder. She had a little extra time on her hands, so she decided to begin reading bedtime stories to some children in a foster home in her area. When she tucked them into bed, she noticed that they were sleeping in the same clothes they had been wearing all day. That's when it dawned on her that these kids didn't have pajamas. The next night, she went out and bought about a dozen pairs of pajamas and marched the kids in one by one so that they could pick out a pair they liked. The expression she saw on those kids' faces that night changed her life. Believing that all kids should have pajamas to sleep in, Genevieve started the Pajama Program in 2001. By the time she appeared on *Oprah* in 2007, she had given away more than eighty-five thousand pairs of pajamas. But the neat thing about the show was that in a secret challenge, Oprah had previously asked her three hundred audience members to bring pajamas with them when they came to the show. There was one catch: they could only buy one pair—the rest they had to raise. What happened on the show that day was amazing. The audience of about three hundred people brought thirty-two thousand pairs of pajamas. Pajamas were everywhere on the show, and as I watched, I felt like they were having church. So you may say it's just pajamas, but I say that for those kids, it's a whole new way of sleeping.[2]

It's just prayer, but don't tell that to Jonathan. I met Jonathan at a camp about ten years ago. He wasn't the kind of kid who would wow anyone with his gifts, talents, or abilities. In fact, he did well just to get a few words out. Jonathan suffered from epilepsy, and his body had seizures literally every minute. Hundreds of seizures a day made it hard for him to control his body. But into this malfunctioning little body God put a fully functioning heart. I remember watching him pray at camp the first night we were there. He struggled for words, but there was something genuine about his intercession. I'll never forget the moment a few nights later when Jonathan came to me off stage and asked me to pray with him for the people in the room who did not know Christ. On some back steps where no one could see us, we knelt down and asked God to work that night. A day later, God took hold of my life by reminding me of Jonathan's heart. Now I've told his story to you. You might say it's just a prayer, but I say it's one way that God is changing the world.

So what is in your hands? What might it look like for Jesus to do the impossible through you? Come on. It's just lunch. Why not give it a try?

12:2∞ Here's Your Challenge— by Now You're on the Clock

By 12:28 tomorrow, fill in the blank. It's just _____. Ask God to show you what gift, talent, ability, or passion He has given you and what you can do with it. Then pass the piece by filling in the blank and watching what God can do with whatever you have to give Him.

DAY 5: Heaven Comes to Earth

by Chris Brooks

I live in a townhome with my family. It's a nice townhome. Our neighbors are an eclectic collection of characters. But with a growing family, a backyard smaller than a sandbox, and an English bulldog that poops like a dump truck, our little piece of the American dream can feel a bit crowded sometimes. So we are house hunting.

I want to live in a subdivision called Wilson Ferry that is just across the street from our townhome community. It has bigger houses and nice, open backyards that I bet my bulldog would love. It has a community pool, tennis courts, and an indestructible community center you can rent out for your kids' birthday parties so that their friends don't trash your house. It's paradise, as far as I'm concerned.

So my family and I drive through Wilson Ferry a lot, daydreaming of what house we would like to live in and what our lives would be like if we lived there. I can even picture my kids behaving better just because there is a pool in our neighborhood. We may not ever say it out loud (Okay, maybe I said it once) but it's almost as if we believe we would be a better family if we lived in a better neighborhood. Sometimes I can get so wrapped up in dreaming about and driving through Wilson Ferry that I neglect my townhome, ignore my current neighbors, and treat my family as an inconvenience until we get into our new home.

John 14:1–4 (The Voice):

Jesus: Don't get lost in despair; believe in God and keep on believing in Me. My Father's home is designed to accommodate all of you. If there were not room for everyone, I would have told you that. I am going to make arrangements for your arrival. I will be there to personally greet you and welcome you home, where we will be together. You know where I am going and how to get there.

In this passage, Jesus was trying to comfort His disciples by showing them a piece of what the kingdom of God fully realized looks like and feels like. The disciples were getting antsy about following Jesus while still being trapped in the townhome of their present existence. Like them, we know that Jesus will make all things new and that heaven is coming to earth. But the trap we can fall into as Christians is spending so much time thinking about when and how we will get transported out of our bad neighborhood here on earth and into a better one in heaven that we neglect our God-given responsibility to pass the piece. I can easily fall into the trap of treating this earth and other people like my townhome—as just a temporary situation that we can ignore because we would rather think about what our new home might be like. But perhaps the best way to view it is that our lives, our bodies, and this earth are one day going to get the greatest renovation ever.

Keeping the joy of heaven before you is right and good, but only as much as it impacts your life and your actions here and now. This is the point to which the *Domino Effect* has been pushing—helping you grasp the full story of God so that you can partner with Him in writing new chapters where the characters live out the story of good overcoming evil every day.

Maybe one day my family will be able to get a house in Wilson Ferry. But my role as a husband, a father, and a neighbor is to create a home that overflows with love, hope, and mercy right now—regardless of where I live.

12:28 Here's Your Challenge— Now You're on the Clock

By 12:28 tomorrow, renovate. Take inventory of the people or causes or places in your life that need to be renovated. Who have you overlooked? What have you turned your back on? Realize that you are an active agent of redemption and that you will be a participant in the resurrection, and then bring that power to a place in your life that needs it the most. Cultivate your home here and now so that you'll be ready when heaven comes to earth.

Notes

Session 01
1. Gene Weingarten, "Pearls Before Breakfast," http://www.washingtonpost.com.
2. Ellen Goodstein, "8 Lottery Winners Who Lost Their Winnings," MSN Money.

Session 02
1. "Somewhere over the Rainbow," Wikipedia, http://en.wikipedia.org/wiki/Over_the_Rainbow.

Session 04
1. Malcom Gladwell, *The Tipping Point* (New York: Back Bay Books, 2002), 28.
2. http://www.quotedb.com/quotes/1905.

Session 06
1. www.tomsshoes.com/ourcause.aspx.
2. www.pajamaprogram.org/purpose.html.